C000179238

25
Dresses

Iconic moments in twentieth-century fashion

William Banks-Blaney
WILLIAMVINTAGE

QUADRILLE

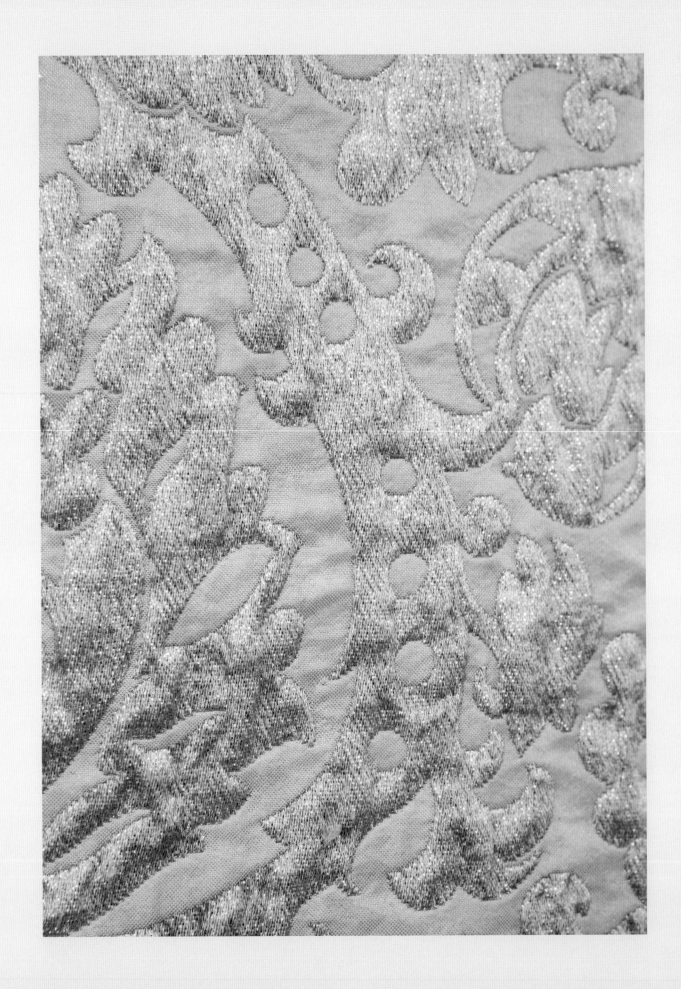

RACHEL ZOE IN A JEAN PATOU HAUTE-COUTURE DRESS, 1967
PHOTOGRAPHED BY JUSTIN COIT

Foreword

I first met William when he invited me to a private appointment at his store in London. It was my first time setting out to shop since my son Skyler was born and walking into William's store was like stepping into a dream.

It was one of the most extraordinary vintage stores I had ever been to, filled with countless iconic designer vintage treasures from Dior haute couture and Pierre Cardin to André Courrèges and Geoffrey Beene. William knew the detailed history and inspiration behind every single piece without even blinking and, as someone who has been collecting vintage for more than two decades, I had never met another person who shared the same infectious passion for it as I did. Accompanied by my husband and son, we spent the entire day shopping and we found ourselves swapping our espressos for wine, as morning breakfast turned into afternoon lunch. I will never forget that day; it was the longest I've ever spent in one store and William's impeccable taste and eye for spotting the most unique and special pieces from around the world were like nothing I had ever seen. After that day, William and I quickly became vintage soulmates and lifelong friends.

William possesses an insurmountable knowledge of vintage. He is truly an encyclopedia of couture and one whose passion is equal to his acclaimed expertise. In addition to his countless talents, William has a remarkable spirit which is reflected in how he lives his life and his relentless approach to his work; his sophistication and polish are evident all the way down to his unique style. It is only fitting that William's first tome is broken down into beautifully illustrated chapters incorporating designers both past and present. Immerse yourself in the journey of *25 Dresses* with William, as he shares his expertise in fashion and pays homage to the history of couture over the decades. I hope this book inspires you to celebrate the history of vintage and appreciate the important role it plays in fashion today.

Rachel Zoe

"William possesses an insurmountable knowledge of vintage. He is truly an encyclopedia of couture."

Introduction

Whether you are a dedicated follower of contemporary fashion or a vintage devotee, I hope *25 Dresses* inspires you. I hope this book demonstrates how the 'language of fashion' is something as old as time itself and is a language that can be learned by anyone. More importantly, I hope it shows how fine vintage clothing is not simply a gateway to the past but that it is the lifeblood of fashion in the twenty-first century.

My role in fashion is one not born from years of specialist training, but rather something that happened by chance. Previously an interior designer, I regularly stumbled across wonderful pieces of vintage clothing on buying trips. Often forgotten and relegated to a dusty shelf, I found dresses that were extraordinarily modern and yet might be fifty or more years old. These neglected treasures were pieces I knew others would adore and, after years of giving these discoveries to delighted friends as gifts, I saw a gap in the market for an edited collection of the best examples of vintage clothing for the modern woman.

WilliamVintage was initially launched as a series of pop-up sales. I recall the first nerve-wracking sale for fifty friends; it was a sell-out. At the fourth pop-up sale, over four hundred women bought vintage clothing for the first time in their lives and, inspired by such an extraordinary response, the WilliamVintage store soon followed. Over the years, it has given me great pleasure to see my discoveries so eagerly sought after and chosen by the most extraordinary women.

I cannot begin to thank sufficiently Tilda Swinton, Emma Thompson, Sally Hawkins, Gillian Anderson, Kate Upton, Lily Allen, Jessie J, Lana del Rey and many more for choosing WilliamVintage. It is a huge source of pride to see dresses I have unearthed feature so prominently within the pages of the most celebrated publications. With the support of Lucinda Chambers at British *Vogue* and Katie Grand at *LOVE*, WilliamVintage discoveries have been photographed by Patrick Demarchelier, Jean-Baptiste Mondino, Tim Walker and Nick Night while modelled by Kate Moss, Edie Campbell, Karlie Kloss and Jean Campbell.

While the foundation of WilliamVintage is the finest vintage haute couture and our client list includes the world's most famous women, designers, museums and archives, I have never been a label snob. If a dress appeals to me and I think it remains relevant, I will move mountains to make sure it becomes a WilliamVintage piece irrespective of its monetary value. The key to a truly timeless piece of vintage clothing is that it remains pertinent to the modern wardrobe, and no one understands this better than my great friend Rachel Zoe. Rachel has been a constant source of inspiration and encouragement since we first met in the newly opened WilliamVintage store and bonded over a 1950s Yves Saint Laurent dress. Her passion for fashion and for vintage haute couture is matched only by her passion for living life to the fullest and, in that, Rachel is the essence of the WilliamVintage woman.

I hope that you enjoy reading *25 Dresses* and that within these pages you discover the magic of vintage haute couture.

William Banks-Blaney

1

Fortuny

and the
Charioteer
of Delphi

The 'Delphos' dress created by MARIANO FORTUNY is one of the most iconic designs in the world and has been a source of inspiration for more than a hundred years.

A Fortuny Delphos is perhaps the most celebrated dress ever designed, yet seemingly it is no more than a sheath of silk with a simple belt. First created in 1907, this fabled garment and an exemplar in design and construction should be viewed in the context of early Edwardian fashion. The beginning of the twentieth century was a time of strict tailoring and corsetry, when the shape of a woman was manipulated and suggested but never fully expressed and which still clung in many ways to Victorian sensibilities. The Delphos was in the vanguard of change. As revolutionary as its design and construction was the way in which it was to be worn; the sole item upon the body with no undergarments whatsoever, so a woman's natural beauty and organic lines could be clearly seen. The Delphos was deemed so daring that it could only ever be worn within the home.

Mariano Fortuny came from a wealthy, educated and erudite family. His father was a successful painter who had won the Prix de Rome and counted Queen Isabella of Spain as a patron while his maternal grandfather was also an adept artist who had been formally educated at the École des Beaux-Arts in Paris. The family was well travelled and avidly collected textiles, art and metalwork from around the world and across the centuries for personal inspiration. Mariano Fortuny was born into this creative, eclectic world in Spain in 1871. The family relocated to Paris when Fortuny was three, before deciding to make Venice their permanent home when he was eighteen, establishing themselves in a grand Renaissance palazzo. Displaying a passion for art and textiles at an early age, this formative period for Fortuny explains how he evolved into the man christened 'The Magician of Venice'.

While the Delphos dress has become Fortuny's most famous work, he never considered himself a fashion designer. A metalworker, painter, lighting engineer and textile

ABOVE: THE CHARIOTEER OF DELPHI, 474BC

BELOW: MRS CONDÉ NAST IN HER FORTUNY DRESS, c1912

OPPOSITE: A WILLIAMVINTAGE FORTUNY DRESS IN BLACK SILK WITH ITS ORIGINAL SILK BELT, c1918

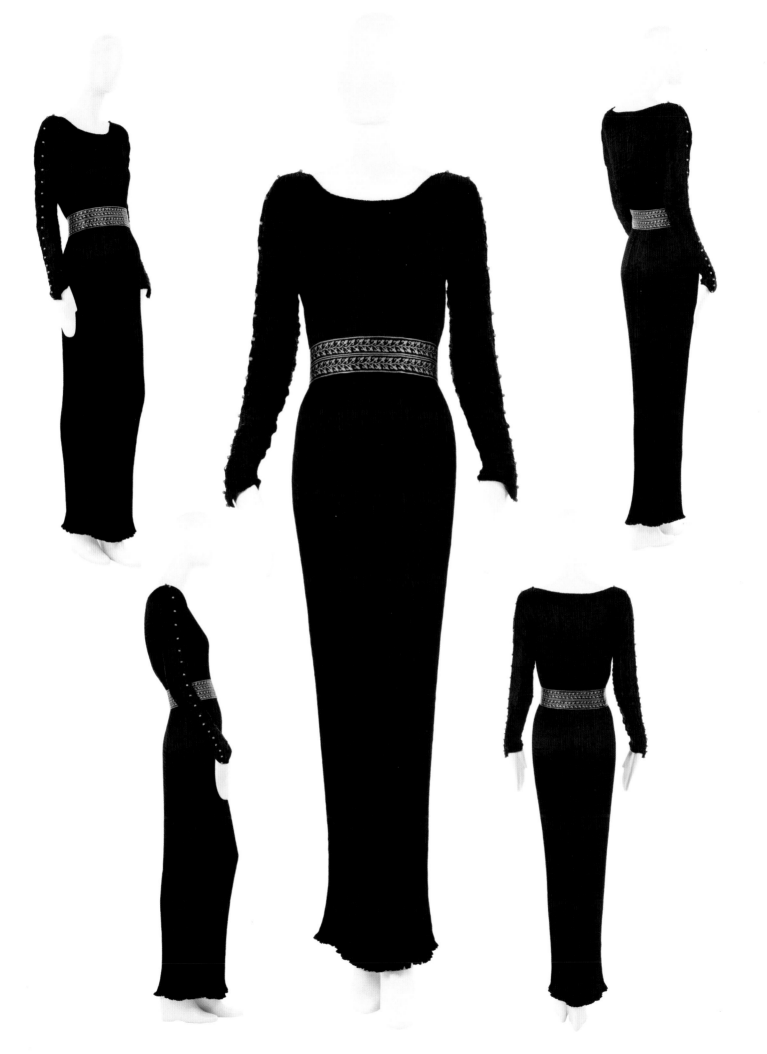

obsessive, Fortuny registered over thirty patents during his lifetime. One of his greatest inventions was the technique with which his Delphos dress was created; the unique micro-pleating of silk is a process still veiled in mystery, which despite myriad attempts to recreate, has never been mastered by anyone else. Fortuny was the definition of a 'Renaissance Man' who sought knowledge, inspiration and development from his surroundings and from all corners of the globe. His designs were influenced by Arabic, Italian, Chinese, Greek, Egyptian and Hawaiian art, many examples of which were contained within his family's extensive private collection. The Delphos dress, however, in both design and nomenclature, has a clear source: The Charioteer of Delphi.

The Charioteer of Delphi is widely regarded as the greatest example of Early Classical Greek sculpture dating to c478BC. While our twenty-first-century eyes have become used to museums displaying such statues expertly lit and wonderfully exhibited, ever since their discovery during the classical excavations of the seventeenth and eighteenth centuries, The Charioteer is a very different entity. Discovered by chance under a rockfall, it was excavated as late as 1896 and its extraordinary condition, quality and lifelike rendering created a furore when Fortuny was an inquisitive, artistic fifteen-year-old starting to develop a lust for the ancient world. The immediacy of discovery is a powerful thing and The Charioteer was not something Fortuny stumbled upon one day in a museum; it was making headlines around the world and its bright glass eyes, solid silver eyelashes and extraordinary bronzework would have appealed to everything the Fortuny family and the young Mariano were passionate about.

Ten years later, it comes as no surprise that Fortuny created a garment he named the Delphos. Quickly proving popular with a monied, educated and liberal clientele, a Delphos dress was coveted by princesses and performers alike. It appealed not just because of its rare comfort and sinuous form but because it spoke of the ancient world and of a romantic approach to history; its very creation was known to be shrouded in secrecy, both artisanal and mysterious.

The first women to wear a Delphos fully embraced the Hellenic look, wearing the dress with coiled hair and primitive

OPPOSITE: TINA CHOW IN ONE OF HER FORTUNY DRESSES PHOTOGRAPHED BY ANTONIO LOPEZ, c1975

RIGHT: A WILLIAMVINTAGE FORTUNY DRESS IN APRICOT SILK WITH ITS ORIGINAL SILK BELT, c1912

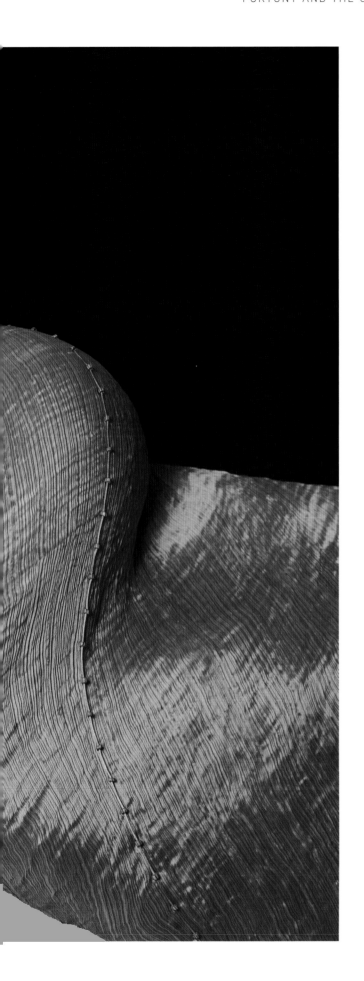

'The Delphos became the wearable, revolutionary garment that expressed not only a desire to celebrate the female form, but also intellectual sophistication.'

jewellery. In the sepia photographs of the early twentieth century, these women resemble statuary all the more, seeming lifeless and unbreathing. It is only on seeing a Delphos dress in colour that its true magic becomes clear; bright, jewel-like tones in shimmering silk that seem to have a life of their own reveal another key element of the Fortuny approach to creation. To obtain the colours that so inspired him from his family's collections, through his father's and grandfather's paintings, and through living in saturated Venetian light, Fortuny created all his own pigments from mineral and vegetable compounds and was known to dye his silks more than fifteen times to achieve the rich hues he desired. The colours of a Delphos dress are joyous, fantastical and speak of colours now lost to us, made as they were from turmeric and cardamom, lapis lazuli and cobalt. Even a black Delphos has an iridescence more like a raven's wing than the flat tones of night.

While Fortuny grew up in the late Victorian age with its often dour and heavily medievalised obsessions, his family's painterly approach was grounded in the Romantic movement; in colour, light and nature the Delphos was the incarnation of this very different artistic approach. First seen through the prism of the Pre-Raphaelite school, the medieval past was being literally lightened and refracted by a more pagan approach, bringing in elements of classical antiquity, dream-like visions and portraits of women who were more ethereal goddesses than corporeal beings. The Delphos saw the movement come full circle and it became the wearable, revolutionary garment that expressed not only a desire to celebrate the female form as worshipped by an artist, but also an intellectual sophistication that has remained as indelibly linked to the dress as its unique production.

LEFT: GLORIA VANDERBILT IN ONE OF HER FORTUNY DRESSES, PHOTOGRAPHED BY RICHARD AVEDON FOR VOGUE, 1969

After the deaths of Mariano Fortuny in 1949 and then his wife Henriette in 1965, production of the Delphos dress ceased as its secrets were lost and, more romantically, because it is said Fortuny wanted the Delphos to exist only while his wife was alive. Despite this, the impact of the Delphos, its role within fashion and its artistic perfection continue to inspire design in the twenty-first century. Mary McFadden sought to re-create the Fortuny magic in the 1980s and produced a version of the arcane Fortuny pleating. However, it was only achievable when heat-treating synthetic fibres, the ability to do so in silk still proving impossible to all who tried. In 1993 the avant-garde designer Issey Miyake directly referenced the genius of Fortuny with his first 'Pleats Please' collection. Whether by commercially successful designers like Mary McFadden, Issey Miyake or Romeo Gigli, or by graduates of Parsons and Central Saint Martins, the Delphos dress is honoured throughout fashion, either in attempts to replicate its extraordinary execution or to reinterpret its language anew.

More extraordinarily, the Delphos dress has never become *démodé*. Produced from 1907 until 1960, with only minute variances in design during that time, it has been a wearable piece of clothing within every decade since its inception.

From its birth as the leitmotif for an educated mindset and referenced continuously by Marcel Proust in *À la Recherche du Temps Perdu*, it weathered the Roaring Twenties with its Venetian glass beads, it survived the Art Deco desires of the 1930s with its pared-back simplicity and sinuous lines, and it proved the counterfoil to Dior's New Look and the fast-paced changes of the Parisian couture houses during their golden age. The Delphos can be glimpsed, like a rare bird, throughout the pages of fashion history, whether photographed upon Mrs Condé Nast in 1919, Mai Mai Sze in 1934, Gloria Vanderbilt in 1969, Tina Chow in 1977, Lauren Bacall in 1978, Natalia Vodianova in 2009 or Tilda Swinton in 2013. The story of the Delphos dress is as much a part of the history of art as it is a part of the history of fashion but, above all, it is a part of the history of women.

OPPOSITE: MAI MAI SZE WEARING ONE OF HER FORTUNY DRESSES, PHOTOGRAPHED BY GEORGE PLATT LYNES, 1934

The Fortuny Legacy

JW Anderson

Proenza Schouler

Oscar de la Renta

Chanel

2

The Flapper's Folly

There are few dresses as redolent of the era in which they were made as they are of their designer. This spectacular haute-couture creation by GABRIELLE 'COCO' CHANEL is one of the greatest.

Christened the 'Ribbon Dress' by Chanel in 1924, this is generally regarded as being one of the world's first 'Little Black Dresses'. In a swathe of black silk and a shimmer of glass, this dress evokes the Roaring Twenties, the flapper and the age of Art Deco. Still spectacular to our twenty-first-century eyes, the dress created headlines in both British and French *Vogue* when it debuted in Paris and in August 1924 *Women's Wear Daily* described it as:

One beaded evening dress that will probably be much seen about ... cut with the deep U neckline at back and a less deep one at front that is the favourite décolletage here this season. Its skirt has two or three layers of the crêpe from waist to about knee-line slit into half-inch wide fringes of irregular lengths that are weighted down by being covered with jet bugles. The effect is a very graceful dress.

Created from the finest black silk georgette, the dress is expertly layered and composed of a slip dress with a ribboned, beaded skirt and a beaded tunic that sits upon it, both of which separately are entirely transparent. It is only when the two are worn in unison that the magic of Chanel's Ribbon Dress comes to light: a sparkling, sinuous dress that sways rather than floats and while composed of numerous layers of silk and glass has within it an intense, body-skimming eroticism and sense of imminent reveal. The black-glass bugle beading, set tightly on each of the many hundreds of ribbons, leads to a design at the midriff that is often considered to be Aztec in inspiration but is just as much a story of a metropolitan skyline and the skyscrapers being erected throughout the Roaring Twenties.

The 1920s was a period of optimism and celebration following an event that changed the face of international relations forever: the First World War. It is impossible to imagine living in a world where England, Ireland, Scotland, Wales, America, Russia, China, France, Germany, Austria,

ABOVE LEFT: THE EMPIRE STATE BUILDING DESIGNED BY WILLIAM F LAMB, 1929–31

LEFT: A FASHION ILLUSTRATION FOR FRENCH VOGUE, APRIL 1926

OPPOSITE: A WILLIAMVINTAGE CHANEL RIBBON DRESS IN BLACK SILK GEORGETTE WITH BLACK GLASS BUGLE BEADS, 1924

Belgium, Serbia, Portugal, Brazil, Romania and over twenty more countries took part in a four-year battle that decimated Europe and saw more than sixteen-million deaths and twenty-million serious injuries. By the end of the conflict in November 1918, the Russian and Austro-Hungarian imperial empires were no more and the map of Europe had to be redrawn as new territories and new countries emerged. It is only with hindsight that we call this event the First World War; those who survived it believed nothing of its kind could happen again and so it was simply known as 'The Great War'.

With many émigrés having fled German troops or Russian Bolsheviks and finding new homes, a desire to rebuild and renew was expounded on a global scale. Artists and aristocrats, masons and musicians, princes and paupers all changed allegiances; cities were rebuilt, art and music flourished, and The Great War marked a point of change from the previously corseted and often claustrophobic ethos of the Edwardian era. The start of the twentieth century had still been encumbered by much of the nineteenth-century coda for how to live one's life and in the aftermath of the war, following so much death, a desire to make light, make happy and live well was cultivated. It was this sense of fleeting joy that led to the iconic flapper girl and the world in which she lived.

Chanel's designs throughout the 1920s have long been associated with the emergence of the flapper and the early Art Deco movement. Her haute-couture pieces garnered world press and a following by the richest women on earth. Never one to undervalue herself or her clothing, Chanel's haute couture was always the most expensive clothing in the world and her impeccable designs and high prices meant there was no other label as aspirational or glamorous. The Chanel obsession was all the more powerful given that her designs were seen to be so daringly modern. Whilst her contemporaries Jeanne Pacquin, Jacques Doucet and Charles Worth struggled to inspire women in the 1910s and 1920s, it was Chanel's untrained approach to fashion and her understanding of women that set her apart as much as her exquisite taste. Soon her designs were being copied and used as inspiration for women around the world, with Chanel-style flapper dresses being sold in boutiques and department stores everywhere.

By the 1920s not only had most of Europe and America triumphed in The Great War but so too had women fighting

OPPOSITE: MARION MOREHOUSE IN CHANEL HAUTE COUTURE, PHOTOGRAPHED BY EDWARD STEICHEN, FEBRUARY 1925

OVERLEAF: MARION MOREHOUSE IN CHANEL HAUTE COUTURE, PHOTOGRAPHED BY EDWARD STEICHEN, 1926

for female liberation. From being contained and constrained only 20 years previously, women had been granted the right to vote in Norway in 1915, Denmark in 1916, Britain in 1918, the Netherlands in 1919 and America in 1920. The first quarter of the twentieth century saw enormous change in women's rights. The flapper was perceived as the twentieth-century woman incarnate; drinking, driving, partying, voting and speaking her mind. The term itself, however, was initially used as a criticism, rather than as a compliment, by those who viewed this change as being more of a problem than a freedom. Just as women's rights were changing, so too were their wardrobes and it was this shift in psyche that Chanel had identified before the war. Chanel loathed the idea of a woman being unable to dress herself, to have to be fastened into corsets and bustles, to be unable to drive or to move freely. Throughout her working life, she never lost sight of designing clothes that would enhance not only a woman's figure but also her life. This dress is a superb example of both her approach and the new freedom of fashion in the 1920s: a gossamer-thin dress that skims the body rather than constrains it and that, with an artful shrug of the shoulder, could leave the wearer naked.

When Chanel was designing the Ribbon Dress in her atelier in the rue Cambon in Paris in 1924, F Scott Fitzgerald was writing *The Great Gatsby*, which was published the following year. Set in Long Island in 1922, the novel has at its core the hedonistic abandon of the Roaring Twenties, the super-rich and the flapper girl. While the life depicted within its pages shows the stupendous wealth resulting from the economic boom of the 1920s, the celebratory spirit of the post-war years and the Jazz Age in all its glory, it also reveals how living for nothing other than pleasing oneself had its curses. Daisy, Gatsby's great love and the ultimate flapper girl with her parties, her money and her $300,000 pearl necklaces, hints at this sense of sadness underneath the glamour when talking of her newly born daughter. 'I hope she will be a fool; that's the best thing a girl can be in this world, a beautiful little fool.' *The Great Gatsby* is now considered not only as a great work of American literature but also the linchpin novel of the 1920s, the fascination with the era and the romantic, hedonistic ideals within it resulting in two major films, in 1974 and 2013, both of which brought about major revivals in 1920s style.

So much has been written about the house of Chanel and the private life of Gabrielle Chanel that one can often lose the magic and immediacy of a dress when trying to categorise a legend. At the time 'Coco' Chanel was designing this dress she had lost the fabled love of her life, 'Boy' Capel, only four years previously. She had launched her first perfume, Chanel

Number 5, with her inheritance from Boy and still mourning his death she had embarked upon an affair with Grand Duke Dmitri Pavlovich of Russia only to end it for a relationship with Hugh Grosvenor, Duke of Westminster and one of the wealthiest men in the world. She had climbed from abject poverty in South West France and through a series of well-connected lovers and patrons, had ensured her dreams could be made real. When designing this dress, Chanel stood in her atelier in the heartland of Paris as a forty-year-old woman with her name in *Vogue* and her reputation assured as the world's most influential woman in fashion.

While the house of Chanel would continue to evolve and prosper, not so the flapper and the Jazz Age. The economic boom that fuelled the 1920s under the Hoover administration was more smoke and mirrors than hard cash and in 1929, the Wall Street Crash changed the face of America and in turn the world. Tycoons lost fortunes, middle America lost everything and from 1929 to 1932, over 50,000 suicides were recorded in America alone as people could no longer face the destitution left by the crash. The Great Depression of the next ten years changed the playing field in every industry with the realm of haute couture being hit hard. While the Art Deco style of the latter part of the Roaring Twenties survived in a more subdued form, the flapper was a term already considered out of date and inappropriate by 1933.

The impact of 1920s fashion and of Chanel's many extraordinary designs from this period are almost too many to mention; a love affair with all things twenties seemingly taking place at some point in each decade since its close. From the 1970s revival of 1920s fashion brought about by the first Gatsby movie and made flesh by Bill Gibb, Biba and Ossie Clark to the more obvious and direct flapper designs inspired by the second Gatsby movie, the notion of the flapper and her Chanel dresses are inked indelibly upon the heart of fashion and with good reason; they speak of freedom, of joy and of a desire to express the wearer and not the designer.

The Chanel Legacy

Roberto Cavalli *Baby Phat* *Lanvin* *Gucci*

Lanvin

The Ages
of Woman

ABOVE: A PORTRAIT OF MADA PRIMAVESI BY GUSTAV KLIMT, 1912

BELOW: A PORTRAIT OF ADELE BLOCH-BAUER BY GUSTAV KLIMT, 1912

OPPOSITE: A WILLIAMVINTAGE LANVIN ROBE DE STYLE IN EMBROIDERED SILK, c1924

The house of LANVIN has shaped 125 years of change in fashion design and the role of women in society; it is the oldest couture house in Paris.

To understand the secret behind its success and also its magic, one need only look at the logo of the house of Lanvin, which depicts a mother and child hand in hand. While this is a portrait of Jeanne Lanvin and her beloved daughter, Marguerite Marie-Blanche, it is also the embodiment of a journey from girl to woman. It is this journey that was the key to the success of Jeanne Lanvin and to the emergence of perhaps the most artistic, humanist couture house of all time. This fine silk dress with its romantic, ethereal language, delicate embroidery and exaggerated silhouette, is both illustrative of all the hallmarks of Lanvin and an iconic example of the *robe de style* for which she became so famous. Her approach to design, and in particular to the *robe de style*, is perhaps best expressed by Jeanne Lanvin herself: 'My dresses are not premeditated; I am carried away by feeling.'

Born into a working-class family as one of eleven children, Lanvin started her career as an apprentice milliner before training as a dressmaker in the house of Talbot. With the support of one of her clients, she established her own small millinery workshop, which drew increasing patronage from wealthy Parisian women. In 1889 the house of Lanvin was opened, with a more polished atelier; while Jeanne still focused on bespoke hats, her artistic eye and talent were now noted by the *beau monde* of Paris. A marriage to the aristocratic but impoverished Count Emilio di Pietro resulted in the birth of Lanvin's only child, Marguerite Marie-Blanche, and ended in divorce in 1903. However, it was the birth of Lanvin's daughter that became the defining moment of her life, both personally and professionally.

Following the divorce from Count di Pietro, Lanvin found herself in the socially unacceptable and rather lonely place of being a single mother trying to run her own business. Her love for her daughter was translated into the creation of exquisite clothing for her, inspired by Lanvin's passion for seventeenth- and eighteenth-century painting, literature and sculpture. When Lanvin's clients saw the young Marguerite in these unique dresses they placed orders first for their own children and then for themselves. The fashion house of Lanvin had

ABOVE: A PORTRAIT OF MARIE-ANNE CUPIS DE CAMARGO BY
NICOLAS LANCRET, 1730

OPPOSITE: AN ILLUSTRATION FOR LA GAZETTE DU BON TON BY
PIERRE BRISSAUD, 1921

been born from the relationship between a mother and her
daughter, and in 1909, now focusing on clothing for both
women and children, Lanvin was admitted into the Chambre
Syndicale de la Haute Couture.

The house of Lanvin differed from other ateliers not only
in its production of children's clothes alongside women's,
but also in the way the house was funded and managed.
Unlike the aristocratic couture house of Lucile, founded and
funded by Lady Duff-Gordon, the male-dominated houses of
Doucet, Worth and Poiret, and the investment-led house of
Chanel, backed by Étienne Balsan and 'Boy' Capel, the
house of Lanvin had family at its heart. Lanvin employed all
ten of her siblings within the atelier, and her daughter
remained her muse as she blossomed from child to
debutante, from debutante to woman and finally from young
woman to wife, after marrying and becoming Marie-Blanche,
Comtesse de Polignac.

The house of Lanvin had grown steadily in a period of
immense change, when fashion seemed to jump quickly from
the delicate, formal couture of Callot Soeurs and Doucet
before The Great War to the 'à la garçonne' androgyny
introduced by Chanel in the early 1920s. The shift in direction
was navigated perfectly by Lanvin. Every season, she ensured
her house collections were on trend and relevant to her
customers. Her artistic eye and painterly understanding of
fabric ensured a softness and diffusion that appealed to a
refined, aristocratic and educated woman, who appreciated
not only the finished garment but also the ethic of the house.
As the 1920s developed and Lanvin witnessed a harder, more
brittle edge creeping into the decade, as well as a more
unforgiving approach to the haute-couture silhouette, she
returned to her love of the past. She utilised her extraordinary
personal collection of antique fabrics, paintings and
illustrations, together with the dresses she had made for her
infant daughter, and created an innovative ensemble that
could be worn by a young girl, a debutante, a wife or a
mother: the Lanvin robe de style had been born.

While superficially based on formal court dress of
eighteenth-century France and seventeenth-century Spain,

Lanvin's interpretation of the silhouette seen here brings an infinitely more whimsical, romantic and wearable language to the fore. The colour of this gown, a shimmering tone of cloud blue, marked an iconic and far-reaching moment for the house of Lanvin. While initially inspired by the frescoes of the fifteenth-century Proto-Renaissance painter Fra Angelico, so admired by Lanvin, the shade became so widely associated with her that it became known as '*Bleu de Lanvin*' and is the basis for the colour on the ribbons, boxes and bags of the brand today.

Lanvin appreciated that the full skirt of the *robe de style*, when combined with a gently dropped waist, straight-sided bodice and small, capped sleeve, would appeal not only to the youthful debutante but also to the older woman who sought something that flattered the figure and yet spoke a classical language. While the silhouette may be exaggerated and formal, Lanvin's execution was simple. Using only the lightest of silks meant that the vast underskirts and crinolines previously required could be discarded, allowing the silk to move in a way similar to the unforgiving flapper dresses and tabards of the same period. The huge surface area of the skirt of this *robe de style* also allowed for the delicate embroidery for which the house had become synonymous. Inspired by a great many international cultures through her love of the applied arts, the embroidery on this dress illustrates her understanding of the earlier Vienna Secession movement, founded by Gustav Klimt and Josef Hoffman, which was the precursor for the Art Nouveau movement still flourishing in Paris at the time the dress was made.

Lanvin's intensely aesthetic eye and her ability to fuse myriad languages and artistic movements together resulted in an approach to design, a passion for colour and an understanding of fabric and texture unlike any other. Her resulting haute couture was emotive, personal and always had as its inspiration the chapters and changes she felt in both her own life and that of her daughter.

OPPOSITE: A LANVIN HAUTE-COUTURE DRESS FOR THE PAVILION OF ELEGANCE, PHOTOGRAPHED BY MAN RAY, 1925

The Lanvin Legacy

Delpozo

Pam Hogg

Paco Rabanne

Vionnet

The Line of Beauty

ABOVE: TOTO KOOPMAN WEARING A VIONNET HAUTE-COUTURE DRESS, PHOTOGRAPHED BY GEORGE HOYNINGEN-HUENE, 1934

CENTRE: THE ROCKEFELLER CENTER PROMETHEUS BY PAUL MANSHIP, 1934

BELOW: SIMONA WEARING A VIONNET HAUTE-COUTURE DRESS, PHOTOGRAPHED BY MADAME D'ORA FOR L'OFFICIEL, FEBRUARY 1935

OPPOSITE: A WILLIAMVINTAGE VIONNET HAUTE-COUTURE DRESS IN BLACK SILK, c1934

The Art Deco movement was the most cohesive artistic expression the world has ever seen. At its apex in the 1930s it was best represented by one designer, couturier MADELEINE VIONNET.

Created from lustrous black silk satin with a cowled neck, gathered shoulders and deep cutaway back, this 1934 haute-couture dress is emblematic not only of the ideals of the period but also of Vionnet's greatest contribution to fashion, the invention of the bias-cut dress. Vionnet saw the potential in cutting fabric on the bias, a technique previously used for finishing collars, hems and cuffs, to create an entirely new way of dressing that was not about something as two-dimensional as a static silhouette, but rather about the fluidity and reality of a dress when worn by a woman.

Born into abject poverty in 1876, Madeleine Vionnet took her first position in fashion as a seamstress at the tender age of eleven. At eighteen she emigrated to London, where she apprenticed at Kate Reilly, one of the many fashion houses that purchased couture in Paris only to copy it for the local clientele. After a successful tenure at Kate Reilly, Vionnet returned to Paris, where she worked first for the couture house of Callot Soeurs and then that of Doucet. Vionnet spoke of her time at Callot Soeurs with fondness: 'Without them I would have continued to make Fords; because of them I was able to make Rolls Royces.' During her employment at Doucet, however, she was often derided for her love of simplicity in clothing. The house of Doucet was famed for its intricate, detailed couture and at a time of tremendous embellishment in the Edwardian era, when a single dress could feature lace, silk, chiffon, cotton, beading, jewelling, layering and corsetry. Vionnet, however, saw the beauty of simplicity. By the time she established her own couture atelier in 1912, Vionnet had worked within two tremendously successful ateliers as their '*Première*' or head seamstress. Copying the work of countless couturiers during her time with Kate Reilly had gained Vionnet an expert understanding of the construction of clothing as she artfully unpicked and analysed all manner of designs.

Following her first mention in *Vogue* in 1919, Vionnet enjoyed tremendous success throughout the 1920s, but it was in 1927 that she launched the first true bias-cut dress and, in so doing, forever changed the way that designers approach fabric. Vionnet had long admired the natural form and an almost overt simplicity, seen in many of her dresses from the

1920s, but with the bias-cut dress she was finally able to create not just simplicity but also the fluidity she had always sought. Vionnet was a long-time admirer of the dancer Isadora Duncan, with her passion for natural movement and emotive dance. Both women gained inspiration from Classical Greece; Duncan adopting the poses and rhythms she saw in ancient sculpture and ceramics, and Vionnet, like Duncan, being inspired by the simplicity and flowing, organic forms of the chiton and the peplos, which gave freedom of movement and fully expressed the contours of the wearer's body beneath.

All clothing before this moment had been executed 'on the rectangular', making as much use of the precious fabric as possible and ensuring that dresses fell in a vertical, columnar form. In one fell swoop, Vionnet changed everything. The bias cut was extraordinarily wasteful and therefore hugely expensive; cutting fabric at forty-five degrees from the leading edge to create the panels required for a dress produced large amounts of waste material. The technique also required fabric to be specially woven at greater widths to provide the final panels required by Vionnet. The finished dresses, however, were a revolution.

With its silk satin caressing the body and gently spiralling around the wearer, this dress is a lesson in languorous chic.

The fabric moulds itself to every line of the body, caressing the curves of breast, hip and derrière, its gentle sheen highlighting those curves all the more enticingly and drawing the eye constantly around the dress. Before the bias-cut dress there was invariably a 'crescendo' to a gown, whether in the form of a train, an embellished panel or a layering of textures and colours however with Vionnet's invention there was no real end to the beauty. Just as a painting is viewed from a static position, yet a sculpture demands to be seen from every angle, Vionnet had created something that not only expressed the wearer, but also engaged the viewer in a three-dimensional, continuous melody of fabric.

The Wall Street Crash of 1929 brought an end to the flapper and the Roaring Twenties. While the fashion industry was hit hard, within the collapse there was a desperate need for fantasy and expression, and the hard glamour of Art Deco

OPPOSITE: A PORTRAIT OF MRS ALLAN BOTT BY TAMARA DE LEMPICKA, 1930

BELOW: THE GREENBRIER HOTEL DESIGNED BY DOROTHY DRAPER, 1946

OVERLEAF: JEAN HARLOW WEARING A VIONNET HAUTE-COUTURE DRESS PHOTOGRAPHED BY GEORGE HURRELL, 1935

fulfilled that need. In the darkest moments of the Great Depression, monuments were erected, with the 1930 Chrysler Building, the 1932 Rockefeller Center and Radio City Music Hall in Manhattan, the 1933 Hoover Building and the 1936 Daily Express Building in London, and the 1937 Palais de Tokyo in Paris, amongst hundreds of buildings that were testament to a stubborn positivity, and the language for that positivity was Art Deco. Just as architecture adopted the style, so too did everything from switch plates to radiator grilles; Vionnet's dresses became the wearable embodiment of the movement with their sensual, dramatic forms and daring sense of modernity and freedom.

Hollywood, and in particular Samuel Goldwyn, realised that in order to survive the Depression, the cinema experience needed to become more escapist than ever before. Set designs became more lavish, the plots more tantalising and the leading ladies more glamorous. Goldwyn signed up Gabrielle 'Coco' Chanel to dress the leading ladies at Metro-Goldwyn-Mayer for the astronomical sum of one million dollars per year. The contract with Chanel soon ended, but Vionnet proved increasingly popular and her bias-cut dresses helped shape the Art Deco notion of the Hollywood 'Screen Siren'. Jean Harlow, Greta Garbo, Marlene Dietrich and Katharine Hepburn all wore Vionnet on film and in life, as did the most famous dancer in the world, Josephine Baker.

Tamara de Lempicka had found fame as a painter in Europe and she obtained numerous portrait commissions on her arrival in America in 1930. In nearly every single female portrait the subject is painted wearing Vionnet's invention, a bias-cut dress, the sculptural qualities of the dress and the erotic qualities of the wearer's body within it uniting in a perfect Art Deco version of Renaissance Mannerism. Vionnet's approval within the arts was sealed further when her design became the dress of choice for Man Ray, the celebrated Dadaist and Surrealist photographer and painter, who saw in its antique roots and modern simplicity the perfect expression for the age.

Despite the extraordinary successes and iconic status built over a thirty-year period, Madeleine Vionnet closed the doors of her house at the outbreak of the Second World War in 1939 and never returned to the world of haute couture. The impact of her work can in no way be underestimated as nearly every dress seen on a red carpet, at a black-tie dinner or in any location where there is a bias cut, a halter neck or a handkerchief hem owes its very existence to her. The final testament to her extraordinary talent lies in the words of other inspirational designers. The great Cristóbal Balenciaga declared, 'Vionnet is my master', Azzedine Alaïa stated that Vionnet is 'The source of everything and the Mother of us all', and Karl Lagerfeld admitted that 'Everybody, whether they like it or not, is under the influence of Vionnet'.

The Vionnet Legacy

Ralph Lauren

Amanda Wakeley

Alice Temperley

Balenciaga

The Master
of Us All

CRISTÓBAL BALENCIAGA
*is, perhaps, the most hallowed
name amongst all fashion
designers, inspiring awe and
an almost religious reverence.*

There are many sweeping statements made within fashion and hyperbole can surround even the most mundane of designers. However, there is one couturier – with a career that spanned seven decades – for whom all the accolades are appropriate: Cristóbal Balenciaga. Christian Dior described him as 'The Master of us all' and Gabrielle 'Coco' Chanel called him 'A couturier in the truest sense of the word ... the others are simply fashion designers'. The appeal of his creations were succinctly explained by Diana Vreeland, the fabled Editor-in-Chief of American *Vogue* during the 1960s: 'In a Balenciaga you were the only woman in the room ... no other woman existed.'

Balenciaga was born in Spain in 1895. His first position was within a tailor's studio in the aristocratic summer resort of San Sebastián when he was only twelve years old. At just twenty-two, and entirely devoted to fashion, he sought out a meeting with Chanel and formed a friendship with her that was to last more than fifty years. By the time he reached thirty, Balenciaga was designing for the Queen of Spain and other members of the royal family.

During this period it was the work of Chanel and her contemporary Madeleine Vionnet that inspired the young Cristóbal. Theirs were the dresses he invested in and, as was the convention at that time, replicated stitch by stitch, interspersing these copies with his own designs as part of the collection each season. This process and a chance meeting with Madame Vionnet truly ignited his creative flame; when the veteran couturier saw Balenciaga's original designs, she was so impressed that she urged the young man to focus exclusively on his own work.

By the time he arrived in Paris in 1937, Balenciaga had

LEFT: A PORTRAIT OF QUEEN MARIA ANNA OF AUSTRIA BY VELÁZQUEZ, 1652

CENTRE: A PORTRAIT OF A WOMAN WITH A FAN BY FRANS HALS, c1650

BELOW: A PORTRAIT OF CATHERINE OF BRAGANZA BY DIRK STOOP, c1661

OPPOSITE: A WILLIAMVINTAGE BALENCIAGA HAUTE-COUTURE SUIT IN BLACK SILK AND SILK VELVET, 1951

established three successful couture premises in Spain. His houses in Madrid, San Sebastián and Barcelona were all tremendously successful and traded under the name 'Eisa', in honour of his mother's maiden name, Eizaguirre. Indeed, were it not for the Spanish Civil War forcing their temporary closure, Balenciaga may never have moved to Paris, the heart of European haute couture. While his extraordinary talent ensured his designs were well received from the outset, at a time when the French haute-couture industry was focused entirely on its nationals, the Spaniard stood out for bringing something entirely different to haute couture. While the Italian Elsa Schiaparelli was renowned for her outré designs and her relationship with the Surrealists and Dadaists, particularly Salvador Dalí and Jean Cocteau with whom she collaborated, Balenciaga brought a richer and more classically opulent language with him, which remained a defining characteristic throughout his career.

It is no coincidence that Cristóbal Balenciaga is often referenced with ecclesiastical language and that many of his clients are described as 'followers'. An audience with

OPPOSITE: A BALENCIAGA SUIT, PHOTOGRAPHED BY HENRY CLARKE FOR VOGUE, 1955

Balenciaga held almost as much significance amongst his hierophants as a meeting with the Pope did to the Catholic faithful. There are numerous accounts of the ways in which women attempted to inveigle a personal encounter; one client famously pretended to faint during a show in the hope that the great man might make an appearance to see to her welfare, but to no avail.

When Balenciaga decided to close his doors forever in 1968, such was the mystical fervour surrounding his house that the news was treated by the media as a matter of international importance. Amongst his devotees, hysterical telegrams were sent and telephone calls were made. Later, when speaking about the day Balenciaga closed, Diana Vreeland recalled that she had been staying with Countess Mona von Bismarck, one of Balenciaga's greatest clients; in Vreeland's words, after hearing the news, 'Mona didn't come out of her room for three days'.

As with any cult, a vital part of the success of the house of Balenciaga lay in the mystery surrounding its leader, and the intensely private Cristóbal was perfectly suited to this role. While other couturiers wooed their clients and courted the international press, offering *bons mots* to whomever would print them, Balenciaga was reclusive. The man who

The Balenciaga Legacy

Gareth Pugh

Rick Owens

Thierry Mugler

A WILLIAMVINTAGE BALENCIAGA HAUTE-COUTURE DRESS
IN PINK SILK, GILDED LEATHER AND CRYSTAL, c1952

Bernard Blossac 57

remained at the forefront of haute couture for nearly fifty years gave only one interview, at the age of seventy-six and three years after he had closed his house. He did not discuss his stellar client list nor focus upon the glories of his career, but rather spoke about his childhood, his family and his Catholic Spanish upbringing. For it is in his upbringing and his cultural roots that the heart of his house lay. Where French couturiers tended to be inspired by the glories of France, the *Ancien Régime* and, in the case of Dior, the frivolity of artists such as Fragonard and Watteau, and the self-importance of Winterhalter, Balenciaga found inspiration in the paintings of Zurbarán, Goya and Velázquez, the form and colour of the Spanish Renaissance, the Catholic religious ritual and the exuberance of flamenco.

If Balenciaga can ever be defined, or his work categorised, it can only be done in terms of a purity of form and construction. While Dior was insistent that each season he produce a different silhouette and hem length, Balenciaga's collections were more of an evolution. Whether admiring one of his dresses that evoke the New Look of the 1950s or one of the sculptural, abstract designs of his last

OPPOSITE: A FASHION ILLUSTRATION OF A BALENCIAGA DRESS BY BERNARD BLOSSAC FOR L'OFFICIEL, 1957

superlative collection in Spring 1968, a direct line can be drawn between the two. Though colour, fit and proportion may have changed, there is a clear path and a shared signature. Just as a painter may develop notions of light and dark, Balenciaga developed the explicit and implicit, of both a dress and a woman's body within it.

The spectacular haute-couture dress from 1952 [see pages 50–1] is a masterwork of Balenciaga. While it follows the language of the New Look espoused by Dior, it is the continuation of a story first begun by Balenciaga in his 1939 Infanta dress, with its pronounced waistline and full, almost ripe, skirt. The curlicues seen on the Infanta have vanished, yet the organic sensibility is still present in the refined winged edge at the bustline. The detail upon the dress has become a scattering of pomegranates, a fruit not only indelibly linked to Spain, but also a device of the Renaissance implying fertility, abundance and sexuality. Constructed of palest pink silk taffeta and with each pomegranate formed of hand-cut, gilded leather inset with a marquise-cut crystal, the dress plays with the sheen of light reflected on silk, gold and glass; for all its formality, the irregularly placed pomegranates give it an air of whimsy. While the dress is far from demure, and has been garnished with glistening, sparkling fruit, it has purity to it – a clean line, a perfectly

The Balenciaga Legacy

Oscar de la Renta

Zuhair Murad

Oscar de la Renta

*A WILLIAMVINTAGE BALENCIAGA HAUTE-COUTURE DRESS
IN CANARY YELLOW GROS DE NAPLES SILK, c1963*

ABOVE: A PORTRAIT OF SANTA RUFINA BY FRANCISCO
ZURBURÀN, c1630

OPPOSITE: A MODEL WEARING BALENCIAGA HAUTE
COUTURE PHOTOGRAPHED BY JOHN RAWLINGS, 1951

or a half-belt. The *semi-ajuste* suit of 1952, the 'tunic-line' collection of 1954 and the 'sack' collections of 1957 and 1958 all became hugely influential and inspired many designers at the time. Amongst those enthralled by these clean-lined and boldly modern examples of haute couture were two of Balenciaga's employees, André Courrèges and Emanuel Ungaro. Both men would go on to found their own couture houses and to be seen as the modernists of twentieth-century fashion. Nonetheless, they owe a great debt to the work of Cristóbal Balenciaga.

One of the finest examples of 1950s Balenciaga haute couture, this suit (see page 47) was created for Aileen Guinness, a woman as famous for her extraordinary waistline as for her considerable fortune – and this suit has the seventeen-inch waist and thirty-six-inch bust to prove it. Formed of lustrous, ribbed Ottoman silk and set with a vast, silk-velvet collar and jewelled buttons, at first glance the ensemble may seem a part of the classic 1950s silhouette, but in the hands of Balenciaga nothing is entirely classical. The vast collar only enhances the minuscule waist, while the Magyar sleeves – so loved by Balenciaga and which required supreme skill to create – are cut from the same piece of fabric as the body of the jacket and are constructed as one with it. While Balenciaga always sought to enhance the body, whether explicitly or implicitly, at the same time he strove to allow for movement. Despite the sleeves being severely tailored to give an astonishingly fitted line, another of his leitmotifs is apparent; inset at each armpit is a diamond of fabric, so that even in such a tight-fitting garment the arm was not restricted.

In the finest and deepest black, the suit is also a superb example of Balenciaga's palette, which seemed to veer from the pastel and sorbet colours seen in Renaissance frescoes to this intense absence of colour, in what Carmel Snow, the Editor of *Harper's Bazaar*, described as 'So black it hits you like a blow ... a night without stars which makes ordinary black seem almost grey'.

While this suit is a superb example of the apex of 1950s haute couture and a masterpiece of the house of Balenciaga, its darkly Gothic glamour and proportions continue to inspire today, most notably in the work of a designer associated with a far more louche approach to fashion, Azzedine Alaïa. Alaïa's personal collection of Balenciaga haute couture is legendary. When looking at his sinuous, dynamic designs that came to represent the early 1980s, with their 'body-con' aesthetic that included hooded dresses and suits with overscale collars, his love of 'The Master' is apparent.

Count Hubert de Givenchy said, 'If I had not known Balenciaga, I might never have discovered the basic truth

shaped, sinuous curve that does not require pleats, folds or froth; despite its obvious opulence, there is an overriding sophistication and simplicity. The early 1950s saw a rapid development of style and confidence at Balenciaga, and while from 1952 he began shifting the focus from waist to hip to back, in countless variations, this dress is a superb and early example of one of the great couturiers. Moreover, it is a design that continues to inspire, from the 1992 ball gown by Thierry Mugler to the recurring forays into the past made by Vivienne Westwood.

In 1952 Balenciaga developed two primary silhouettes within his daywear, one keeping in line with the fitted, form-enhancing New Look sensibility, and the other a design revelation called the '*semi-ajuste*'. The *semi-ajuste* was something never seen before and, in one garment, seemed to blend two schools of thought. A loose back was paired with a more fitted, shaped front, either by the use of tailoring

about fashion ... design doesn't mean adding a flower here or a superfluous detail there. Creating a perfectly simple dress from a single line, that is great design.' With this remark, the symbiotic relationship between Balenciaga and the tall, handsome French aristocrat who would found the house of Givenchy becomes far clearer. Givenchy and his pared-back, chic haute couture may have become synonymous with his muse Audrey Hepburn, but it was Balenciaga whom he worshipped and believed – as did all others – to be the greatest couturier in the world. The haute-couture evening gown designed by Cristóbal Balenciaga in 1963 and constructed from daffodil-yellow Gros de Naples silk (see pages 54–5) shows not only the development of Balenciaga as his house entered the 1960s, but also the impact upon other couturiers at the time and, in particular, Givenchy.

Starkly beautiful, with a graded hemline and waistline elongating the form, and set with only a single bow as an almost token detail, the dress is a precursor to Balenciaga's ultimate abstraction of form and simplicity, the wedding dress from his very last collection in 1968. Continuing to play with volume, the dress has a sharply fitted bodice leading into a skirt that does not skim or attempt to reduce the line of the abdomen, but rather enhance it.

Balenciaga's dresses from this period have often been compared to those depicted in the paintings of Zurbarán. This dress bears a distinct similarity to the one in his portrait of Saint Rufina from c1630, with even the colour being evocative of the esteemed painting by one of the great Renaissance masters.

Closing his doors in 1968, after what was the most sophisticated, iconic and modern collection of his career, and never to return to the couture house, Cristóbal Balenciaga said, 'The life which supported couture is finished. Real couture is a luxury which is just impossible to do anymore'. Given the struggles of haute couture in the 1960s and, with the emergence of prêt-à-porter, the situation only worsening during the 1970s, Balenciaga again seemed to have led the field. As Dior said of the man adulated by Chanel, Givenchy, Courrèges, Ungaro and Alaïa, amongst countless others, 'We follow the direction he gives'.

OPPOSITE: A BALENCIAGA HAUTE-COUTURE DRESS, PHOTOGRAPHED BY IRVING PENN FOR AMERICAN VOGUE, OCTOBER 1965

The Balenciaga Legacy

Ralph & Russo

Rosie Assoulin

Chanel

Charles James

The Original Enfant Terrible

The creations of CHARLES JAMES have been a source of inspiration for designers from Dior to Halston, and his daywear has become part of the very language of fashion.

The life and work of Charles James illustrates the chasm that can lie between commercial success and artistic appreciation and the choice that all too many creators must face. Revered for more than sixty years by designers, museums and lovers of haute couture, Charles James's name is little known outside that rarefied world. Yet his vision was admired by Chanel, Halston, Schiaparelli and Mainbocher, and his creations have been a continual source of inspiration; Dior credited him with inspiring his New Look of 1947 and Balenciaga called him 'the world's best and only dressmaker'.

Born in England in 1906, James was the product of a rare union between a middle-class British soldier and an American heiress; throughout his life this polarity in parental background would be both his saving and his downfall. A taste for luxury and adventure fuelled by his mother's dowry led to a series of failures and financial disasters that were met with disapproval and scorn from his father. Having been expelled from his all-boys school, Harrow, for a 'sexual escapade' when he was just thirteen, he was eventually sent, at the age of eighteen, to his mother's Chicago-based family. His parents hoped this move would encourage their son to become more responsible and enter a career in architecture, but their hopes were dashed in both cases.

After being fired by the architectural firm, James found his metier within fashion, initially working as a milliner. His mother's circle of wealthy, erudite friends became his clients and ambassadors, and by the late 1920s his attention had turned to clothing. With the financial support of his mother and her wealthy family connections, he established a grand atelier in London in 1929, only for it to collapse under bankruptcy after a matter of months. James fled back to America, where, despite achieving great acclaim, he suffered many more similar financial failures during his career.

Despite countless lawsuits, protracted financial disagreements and ghost companies during his forty-year career, James instilled devotion in his clients unlike any other designer; he became their addiction. Best known for his extraordinary ball gowns and dinner dresses, as Halston remarked, 'his dream was to dress the best in the world,' and

ABOVE: A MODEL WEARING DIOR, PHOTOGRAPHED BY TONY FRISSEL, 1951

BELOW: THE MODEL LOUISE STORMONTH, 1954

OPPOSITE: A WILLIAMVINTAGE CHARLES JAMES AFTERNOON DRESS IN BLACK SILK AND SILK GROSGRAIN, c1952

ABOVE: CHARLES JAMES IN FRONT OF THE HOTEL CHELSEA, PHOTOGRAPHED BY BARBRA WALZ, 1976

OPPOSITE: CHARLES JAMES AND FRIENDS WITHIN THE HOTEL CHELSEA, PHOTOGRAPHED BY DICK BALARIAN, 1965

to create, James struggled financially. While his artistic capabilities were never questioned, his approach to commerce was nightmarish for clients and investors alike. During his career he established more than nine companies, many of which were investigated by the IRS and most of which folded due to an obsessional, self-destructive approach that James could not relinquish.

With each of the companies funded largely by his clients, James would agree to design and create up to seven ball gowns for an investor, which would never materialise; worse, he would 'make available' to clients the rare completed dresses that had been commissioned by another. On the strength of his name and creative genius, James would enter into licensing agreements but fail to deliver sufficient design work. He would also tender ideas that were not only impossible for mass-production but that had initially been created for a previously commissioned couture dress; many of his clients were aghast to discover that versions of their exorbitantly expensive clothes were being created for the middle classes.

While living in a series of expensive hotel suites, yet frequently changing his phone numbers, company addresses and names, and fruitlessly agreeing to provide dresses for his valued clients, James would disappoint and fail to honour the vast majority of his obligations. However, his family, friends and, above all, his clients, understood that within the chaos and deceit lay a true passion. James viewed his creations as works of art and, as with a great many artists, the fact that he had been paid for one of his masterpieces did not stop him viewing the piece as forever his, to do with as he pleased. James paid little attention to the needs of his clients and, on the rare occasion a dress would arrive in time for the event for which it had been ordered, his total obsession with form and line often meant that the client would find it impossible to get into. As Diana Vreeland, former Editor-in-Chief of American *Vogue*, observed, 'He would far rather work and rework a beautiful dress ordered for a certain party than have that dress appear at that party.'

The remarkable ball gowns and evening dresses of Charles James are always held up as his greatest achievements and have been a source of inspiration to countless designers. The 'Sirene' dress of 1938 and the 'Balloon' coat of 1956 had a great impact on Alexander McQueen, and the 'Concert' gown of 1948 influenced Gianfranco Ferré at Dior in his 1996 'Passion Indienne' collection (see page 166). However, the daywear designed by James has become so much a part of the language of fashion as to be seen as its foundation. His 1937 padded silk coat has influenced Rick Owens, Rei Kawakubo and Romeo Gigli,

that is precisely what he achieved. James's client list may have included Marlene Dietrich, Elsa Schiaparelli, Gabrielle Chanel and the most famous women in the world, but it also included Babe Paley, Dominique de Menil, Millicent Rogers and other women who were a part of the very highest social echelon, each, by modern standards, billionaires. The James woman was educated and socially accepted everywhere, from the private palazzos of Venice to the White House. Within this most exclusive niche, James was understood to be the greatest couturier of all. For women who were expected to fly to Paris for their couture fittings, one of the greatest surprises was that their 'dream dresses' were often made in New York, by the volatile and capricious James.

This 1952 cocktail dress, in black silk faille and black silk grosgrain, is one of less than a thousand dresses made by James in a career that spanned six decades. With such a slow rate of completion for dresses that were extremely expensive

while his sharp, sculptural tailoring can be seen within the collections of Thom Browne, McQueen and John Galliano, with the Spring 2010 show for Dior being explicitly inspired by James.

This 1952 dress by James has within it evidence of both the past and what would be the future. Only a few years before the dress was designed, the Second World War had had an enormous impact on fashion and the way in which women dressed. A need for utility and informality had brought about a more masculinised approach to clothing, allowing for ease of movement and, crucially, clothing that could be put on without the need for rear zippers and myriad hooks and eyes, and this dress shows the development of that ideal. While having the Jamesian signatures of an integral cantilevered and padded hip to enhance the silhouette and a cut that accentuated every curve of a woman's body, the dress is button-fronted, with a crisp Oxford collar, a three-quarter sleeve with a double cuff, and a trim of grosgrain, once the preserve of men's top hats, jackets and trousers. In this dress, James has adopted the language of men's tailoring to create an elegant dress for the modern woman. Throughout the 1950s, while Dior, Balenciaga and Givenchy would develop a manner of dressing better suited to the modern age, this earlier dress by James is an example of something now known to all, the shirtwaister; a staple of every design house in the world and the epitome of 'day to night' chic.

When looking at James's designs, it is impossible to categorise him or his work; his ball gowns embody the grand age of couture, influenced by the French Empire of the 1820s, while his daywear speaks of the life and travel of the modern woman. Without doubt, his golden period and time of greatest fame was within the 1940s and 1950s, but from his 'Taxi' dress of 1929 through to the bras he designed for his last collection in 1977, his work was searingly modern and so superbly crafted that it has become the benchmark by which most designers measure themselves.

James's lust for perfect cut and form, and his vision and understanding of fabric when creating his masterpieces, led to his position today as one of the greatest couturiers of all time. However, those admirable qualities, when at the expense of sound business management, ensured that James never made his fortune. Unable to understand that perfection would not necessarily equate to great wealth, he died in 1978, alone and penniless, in the shabby downtown hotel in New York City that he had called home for more than fourteen years.

OPPOSITE: CHARLES JAMES BY AN UNKNOWN PHOTOGRAPHER, 1948

The Charles James Legacy

Donna Karan

Céline

Caroline Charles

Dior

The Canvas of Fashion

When the house of DIOR launched its first collection in 1947, one of its many triumphs was to have produced something that instantly became iconic.

Christian Dior created a look that was at once entirely new and seemed to have been dancing in the mind forever, a language both atavistic and familiar. The 'Elisabeth' ball gown of Autumn/Winter 1954, a confection of silk, velvet and tulle d'illusion, is the perfect evocation of the seminal qualities of Dior and his ability to tap in to our dreams – dreams that are seemingly half-remembered yet, through the ateliers of Dior, brought to physical life. To understand this achievement and the way in which, with one show, Dior changed from an unknown designer to a great artistic genius, one need only look at the man himself.

Born in 1905, the son of a wealthy industrialist, Dior enjoyed a life of great privilege, typical of a child of the new mercantile class, with a main family home in Paris and a summer house on the coast of Normandy. Christian was a quiet, scholarly child. Drawn to the arts and with a desire to train as an architect, he faced virulent opposition from his conservative family; his father hoped he would become a diplomat and sent the young 'Tian' to the Institute of Political Sciences. After attending the school, Dior still saw his future in the applied arts and persuaded his father to support him in an altogether different endeavour, an art gallery. At only twenty years of age, his gallery owned works by Paul Klee, Max Ernst, Salvador Dalí, Joan Miró, Alberto Giacometti, Heinrich Campendonk, Georges Braque, Raoul Dufy, Alexander Calder, Maurice Utrillo and Pablo Picasso. It is hard to imagine a small Parisian gallery owned by a young and inexperienced dealer showing such outstanding works and illustrating such an eye for talent. Dior had found his strength and, while his metier would change, it was during these early years while inhabiting the world of painters and sculptors that his understanding of colour, texture and proportion was so finely honed.

ABOVE: A PORTRAIT OF ADELINA PATTI BY FRANZ WINTERHALTER, c1860

CENTRE: A FASHION DESIGN BY CHARLES FREDERICK WORTH, 1865

BELOW: A PORTRAIT OF ELISABETH OF BAVARIA BY FRANZ WINTERHALTER, c1860

OPPOSITE: THE WILLIAMVINTAGE 'ELISABETH' HAUTE-COUTURE BALL GOWN IN BLACK AND IVORY SILK TULLE D'ILLUSION AND BLACK SILK VELVET, AUTUMN/WINTER 1954

While professionally Dior was specialising in the most avant-garde of artists, he also loved the classics and, based in Paris, lived in the shadows of pre-revolutionary France, from the formality of the Palais Royal to the gardens of the Tuileries. Dior would always claim nature as his primary inspiration and referred to the Dior woman as a 'flower woman'. He named his first collection 'Corolle' (meaning 'petals') and his garden at Granville was often cited as inspiring not only much of his couture but also the many scents created by Parfums Dior. It is interesting to wonder what first inspired Dior's love of gardening, and the secret may lie, once more, in art; the grand portraiture of the previous centuries invariably featured an arcadia that can only have fired his imagination as much as the grand, formal dresses of the sitters within it.

When looking at Dior's early notebooks and palettes, one cannot help but draw a parallel with those of an artist. His notes for the collections of 1947 include exhaustive shades of pink – *rose soupir*, *rose français*, *rose givre* and *rose porcelaine*. When trying to encapsulate what he wanted to achieve for the Spring 1948 palette, Dior noted 'all the blues and all the pinks of the sky, from meteors to birds'. His was an artistic, poetic and undoubtedly painterly approach to fashion, and it was from painting that Dior drew his primary inspiration. While his debut collections scandalised as much as they inspired, with their indulgent use of fabric and corseted silhouette, the debt that these dresses owe to the masterworks of the eighteenth and nineteenth centuries cannot be underestimated; the New Look of Dior was, in fact, anything but new.

Every collection designed by Dior held within it a smaller selection of dresses that he called his '*robes Trafalgar*'. These were the dresses that he considered to be at the nucleus of the season and worthy of the greatest adoration, and were invariably his most formal evening gowns, his *robes de grand gala*. While the world of Dior was one of corsetry and of attenuated, exaggerated shaping, his daywear, or '*tailleur*', is perhaps better understood as the distillation of his evening wear, for it was within the Dior *robes de grand gala* that his love affair with the past was at its most obvious.

A great many of Dior's cocktail dresses and dinner dresses were clearly inspired by the eighteenth century. The design and decoration of Sèvres porcelain and Riesener furniture, with their depictions of a formalised nature, had as much impact as the paintings of Boucher, Fragonard and Watteau, with their overscale bows, ruched and padded hips, bawdy displays of embonpoint and a frivolous, coquettish approach to dress. The 'Almee' dress of Spring 1955 features a design almost identical to a Sèvres porcelain pattern of the 1760s, while the 'Romance' dress of Spring 1956 features a repeated banding of bugle

ABOVE: A PORTRAIT OF EMPRESS ELISABETH OF AUSTRIA BY FRANZ WINTERHALTER, 1865

OPPOSITE: THE DIOR 'LA FRANCE' HAUTE-COUTURE BALLGOWN FROM THE AUTUMN/WINTER 1951 COLLECTION, PHOTOGRAPHED BY WILLY MAYWALD

beads nearly identical to the ormolu gadrooning of commodes made by Jean-Henri Riesener in the 1770s. Dior's eye, forever travelling over the details of Parisian architecture and the glories of the *Ancien Régime*, was able to absorb extraordinarily obtuse references and present them in an entirely original context, at once new and subconsciously familiar.

It was with his *robes de grand gala*, his greatest and most valuable dresses, that Dior he came into his own. Extraordinarily expensive, the level of work that went into each dress is staggering. In 1948 *Elle* described a Dior ball gown as 'the most expensive dress in Paris' and recounted a little of what went into its creation: 8 feet of chiffon, 50 feet of crinoline, 36 feet of tulle, 13 feet of taffeta, 213 feet of tulle d'illusion and more than 500 feet of handmade lace. These ingredients were fused together by a team that, as *Elle* put it, consisted of, '350 people on the lace, 120 on the tulle and taffeta, 200 on the thread ... 1 Christian Dior, 2 workroom heads, 2 models, 2 designers, 7 apprentices, 2 assistant seamstresses, 1 head seamstress, 1 head cutter and 1 technical director'. For this dress, and a great many of the *robes de grand gala*, Dior turned not to Marie Antoinette and eighteenth-century France for inspiration, but to the nineteenth century and the formal paintings of Franz Xaver Winterhalter. This German-born artist, appointed court painter to King Louis-Philippe of France, became the most sought-after portrait painter for European royalty of the nineteenth century. His subjects included Queen Victoria of England, Empress Eugénie of France and Princess Leonilla of Russia. His idealised approach suited the Royal courts for being able to convey an imperious, grand and iconic image. It is clear that for Dior the many female portraits executed by Winterhalter held the perfect combination of romanticism and aristocratic disdain that he adored, and which for him represented what a Dior

woman in her grandest ball gown should emulate. It is almost impossible to look at Dior's 'France' ball gown of Winter 1951 without comparing it to Winterhalter's portrait of Empress Elisabeth of Austria and seeing in both the same language of dress: glamorous, imperious, unapologetic and aristocratic.

Dior's countless inspirations come together as one in the 'Elisabeth' ball gown of 1954. Sitting perfectly within the H-line dictated by Dior that season, where the sinuous vertical lines of a woman were enhanced and offset by horizontal banding, the dress has all the extravagance of a Dior construction, with hundreds of yards of tulle set upon vast quantities of silk and crinoline and finished with a series of extravagant velvet bows. Yet for all its mid-century glamour, it has myriad links to the past. The cloud-like tulle d'illusion accentuates the wasp-like silhouette, redolent of the famous Gibson girls of Dior's teen years, combined with the '*cul de Paris*', the rounded derrière that was the height of fashion at the time of Winterhalter and featured in many of his portraits. At once innovative and yet in fashion terms as old as time itself, the 'Elisabeth' ball gown is a shining example of the way in which Dior became not only the greatest couturier in Paris but the master of our dreams.

OPPOSITE: SOPHIE MALGAT WEARING A DIOR HAUTE-COUTURE BALL GOWN, PHOTOGRAPHED BY MARK SHAW, 1953

The Dior Legacy

Giorgio Armani

Ralph & Russo

Dior

The Outrage of the New Look

On 12th February 1947 an event took place that changed the course of fashion and the way women dressed: CHRISTIAN DIOR held his first show.

It caused a global furore. Thousands of telegrams were sent; phone lines between Paris and the rest of the world jammed as journalists called their editors, desperate to be the first to break the news. All present at the show had realised, during that brief but mesmerising hour, that a cataclysmic event had taken place. This dress, designed by Christian Dior for his New York line in 1954, exemplifies everything he espoused within that first collection. In the simplicity and full-bodied elegance of its black silk lies a story that transformed the French economy and prefaced what became known as 'the golden age of couture'.

In 1947 France was recovering from the devastation of the Second World War. Paris was largely unscathed architecturally, but its psyche was fragile after its occupation by Nazi Germany. As mothers, sisters, wives and girlfriends across Europe mourned the deaths of millions of young men, the global economy was sluggish and good times were part of the distant past. For more than five years, while most able-bodied men were away fighting, women in Europe had been forced to forget glamour and instead become the primary workforce. Manning tractors, factories and offices, women had never been as empowered, nor shown so clearly they were the equal of men. Fashion had altered accordingly. The forties' silhouette, with its 'mannish' appearance, exaggerated shoulders and militaristic detailing, was not only a reflection of the home front but also a result of the shortage of luxury fabrics, as mills closed and imports were restricted. After the war parachute silk was reused for knickers and camisoles but, with silk stockings unavailable, women were known to paint their legs with walnut stain to emulate the appearance of pre-war hosiery.

At a time when both fabric and food were under strict rationing, and the notion of Parisian haute couture was at its weakest, Dior launched his 'Corolle' collection. The world gasped at his audacious, extravagant vision of the female sex. Women had lived without the corset for nearly forty years and, following the triumphs of Chanel, Vionnet, Lanvin, Boulanger and other female couturiers of the 1920s and 1930s, clothing had been created with a simpler silhouette that gave women more freedom. With his first collection, referred to as the 'New Look' by *Harper's Bazaar*, Dior placed women back into the corset and a way of dressing more akin to previous centuries.

TOP: AN ILLUSTRATION FROM THE CAHIER DE COSTUME FRANCAISE OF 1771

BELOW: AN ILLUSTRATION OF MOURNING DRESS, 1788

OPPOSITE: A WILLIAMVINTAGE DIOR COCKTAIL DRESS IN BLACK SILK, c1954

*ABOVE: WOMEN PROTESTING IN FRONT OF DIOR'S HOTEL
IN CHICAGO, 1947*

*OPPOSITE: A DIOR MODEL BEING ATTACKED IN THE STREETS
OF PARIS, PHOTOGRAPHED BY WALTER CARONE, 1947*

There can be no doubt that had the war not starved women of sartorial beauty, mystique and sexuality, the house of Dior and its designs would have foundered in a matter of weeks.

Dior disliked the fluid silhouette made popular by Vionnet during the Art Deco years and loathed the dull uniformity of wartime, which had destroyed for him the beauty of women: their curves, pronounced femininity and sexual allure. Speaking about his inspirations, Dior drew parallels with nature: 'I drew women-flowers, soft shoulders, fine waists like liana and wide skirts like corolla.' The corolla of a flower gave the first Dior collection its name. While a vital element of the magic was a new silhouette and hem length each season, ensuring customers had to return to remain *au courant*, the proportions of the New Look were the backbone of each collection. This dress shows not only the vast 'petal' skirt of the New Look – created with countless yards of the finest silk with cambric backing set upon generous tulle underskirts – but also Dior's guiding design principles and evolution, as well as evidence of the financial foundation of the house of Dior and the reason its designs caused an outcry around the world.

The house of Dior was not the creation of a fashion ingénue but the result of an agreement between mature businessmen. Far from being a new face in the salons of Parisian haute couture, by the time of his first independent collection, Dior was a successful designer with nearly twenty years of fashion experience, working first with the couturier Robert Piguet in 1939 and, following the war, at the house of Lucien Lelong. A businessman with strong commercial instincts, Lelong had a great eye for spotting talent and employed a stable of designers to create his haute-couture offerings. Lelong's design team during the 1940s included Christian Dior, Pierre Balmain and Hubert de Givenchy. In 1946, hearing of a new position within the respected but outdated couture house of Philippe et Gaston, Dior met with the owner. It was to be a momentous event, for instead of presenting himself for the job, Dior proposed the creation of an entirely new *maison de couture*. The wealthy owner – Marcel Boussac, textile baron and Chairman of the International Wool Secretariat – decided to finance Dior and ensure his primary business would also benefit from this new couture house.

The marriage of Boussac's money and influence upon Dior, with his romantic notions of a return to pre-war and indeed pre-revolutionary glamour for French women, cannot be underestimated. At a time when a skirt was produced using three yards of fabric, the plainest of skirts from Dior's 1947 collection required twenty yards of wool or silk. The 'Diorama' dress, a signature of the collection, was made of fine black wool, weighed eight pounds and had a skirt circumference of an astonishing forty yards, which in itself caused a furore.

Dior's opulent New Look left women either mesmerised or enraged that after so many years of sartorial freedom, during which they proved themselves capable of working in industry, Dior placed them back on a pedestal as an object of worship, and while doing so made their waists smaller and their skirts longer. The approach was deemed by many to be as constraining as that of eighteenth-century Versailles with complaints that Dior was every bit as decadent as Marie Antoinette. The evocative images of Dior's designs being modelled in the streets of Paris in the 1940s and 1950s capture the imagination today, but such was the outcry against the lavish designs that a Dior model was attacked at one of these photo-shoots. Spotted posing for the camera by French women angry at Monsieur Dior and his fashion dictats that only the supremely wealthy could hope of achieving, the house model had the exuberant, luxurious clothing torn off her back and could only watch as the women ripped it to pieces in protest.

When Dior arrived in America in 1948, fêted as the new King of Couture, there were as many hisses as there were cheers. Banners bearing the slogans 'The Alamo Fell but our hem lines will not!' and 'Mr Dior, we abhor dresses to the floor!' were raised by the Little Below the Knee Club, the League of Broke Husbands of Philadelphia and countless other anti-New Look associations, who saw Dior's designs as nothing less than proof of insensitive consumption. While the removal of fabric rationing in 1948 helped the house of Dior, the Dior client never had concerns about rationing, nor about the propriety of wearing vastly expensive, luxuriant haute couture during one of the most economically dry periods of the twentieth century.

If unable to purchase a real Dior, the average woman nonetheless enjoyed the New Look as it became the basis for every cocktail dress, ball gown and prom dress throughout the 1950s. The iconic Dior cocktail dress remains the byword for jaw-dropping glamour and therein lies the magic of Dior's New Look. It brought lust back into fashion at a time when it had become little more than utilitarian. Irrespective of how much it cost, it reminded women what it felt like to be the most desired object in the world. In a letter to her sister in 1947, Nancy Mitford wrote, 'My life has been made a desert of gloom by the collection which at one stroke renders all one's clothes unwearable... the new house of Dior is for us, boned waists and skirts so long and heavy one can hardly lift them, and for £100.'

From an initial workforce of 85 in 1947, the house of Dior had more than 4,000 by 1953, with more than eight licensed brands available in locations from New York to Casablanca, London to Havana and, of course, Paris. Dior's outrageous, impractical, vastly expensive and uncomfortable clothing had captivated the world, transformed the struggling French economy and placed Paris once again at the heart of fashion.

OPPOSITE: A MODEL WEARING THE DIOR 'BERTHE' DRESS, PHOTOGRAPHED BY WILLY MAYWALD, 1952

The Dior Legacy

Dior *Givenchy* *Adeam*

Balmain

and the
Jewellers of Paris

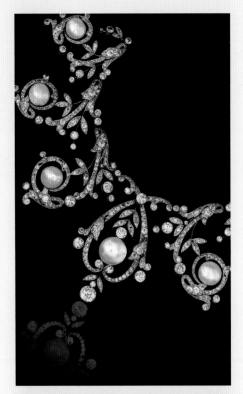

This spectacular haute-couture ball gown from Spring 1954 holds within it every nuance associated with the house of BALMAIN and is one of the greatest surviving examples of its golden age.

Peter Sarstedt's song 'Where Do You Go To (My Lovely)' not only references the work of the great couturier Pierre Balmain by name, but could be an ode to the archetypal Balmain client. The tale of a man watching the woman he loves evolve into a glamorous lady of leisure, with racehorses and a friendship with Picasso, attending soirées at the Parisian embassies, summering in Juan-les-Pins and skiing in St Moritz, is entirely in tune with the lives of the women who adored the magnificent ball gowns with which Balmain made his name.

Constructed in ivory silk satin, with its sinuous lines, flattering décolletage, extraordinarily full skirt and dream-like embroidery, this dress, from Balmain's Spring 1954 collection, conveys far more than merely the stylistic approach of a designer, albeit an exulted one. It holds within it the evolution of Parisian haute couture, the passion and labour of the ateliers, studios and *maisons* of France and the *petites mains* of Paris, whose work would unite to create something of singular beauty and extravagance. There is magic within every piece of vintage haute couture, but the intoxication that results from the marriage of silk, satin, boning, solid-silver thread, seed pearls and hand-cut crystal when under the direction of both the great Pierre Balmain and the legendary embroiderer François Lesage has no equal.

I discovered this dress within a medieval cellar deep beneath the streets of Paris, boxed up decades ago and placed upon a darkened shelf. It was one of a vast number of haute couture gowns commissioned by an aristocratic French family who understood the artistry of haute couture and whose collection, were it ever to see the light of day in its entirety, would set the fashion world aflame. Opening the box and slowly unrolling yard after yard of embellished, sparkling silk, I understood more than ever before not only the pleasure of the highest form of haute couture, but also the excruciating love and obsession required to make such pieces. A dress can be designed, a toile can be created and a bolt of silk can be cut and embroidered, but when an haute-couture dress of this quality is completed, it becomes far greater than the sum of its parts. Alongside the knowledge of the hundreds of hours and dozens of hands it took to bring it to life, and the fortune

ABOVE AND BELOW: NECKLACE AND TIARA WITH NATURAL SEAWATER PEARLS AND DIAMONDS, c1900

OPPOSITE: A WILLIAMVINTAGE HAUTE-COUTURE BALMAIN BALL GOWN IN IVORY SILK WITH SEED PEARLS, PEARLISED GLASS, HAND-CUT CRYSTALS AND SILVER THREAD, c1954

required to pay for it, the dress holds the promise of the night when it would first be worn and how it would make the wearer feel when making her debut. Seeing the dress spread out before me and knowing I had found a fabled gown reminded me of a thank-you letter written by a client to Pierre Balmain and published in 1959 by Ginette Spanier, Directrice of Balmain from 1947–76, in her book *It Isn't All Mink*:

It gave me a taste for life again. Never mind the dress; its sheer arrival was enough, carried by a man in uniform in its enormous new cardboard box, surrounded by pounds of tissue paper. When I signed for it I felt everything was worthwhile and that life was exciting again. Thank you.

The ball gowns of Pierre Balmain were for the very rich indeed and Balmain never pretended otherwise. His reputation had been founded upon the embellished, sparkling dresses that would often incorporate precious metals, semi-precious stones and acres of embroidery. Of the in-house designers at the house of Lucien Lelong, which included Christian Dior and Hubert de Givenchy, Balmain was the first to leave his position to establish his own label, and he was not afraid of opulence. In his Winter 1948 collection, scant years after the end of the Second World War, when both food and fabric were severely rationed, Balmain sent his models out wearing fox stoles with twelve-carat diamonds in place of the animals' eyes.

ABOVE: FRANÇOIS LESAGE, ARMED WITH HIS GUN, WATCHES AS SEAMSTRESSES ATTACH 500 DIAMONDS TO A COUTURE DRESS, PHOTOGRAPHED BY MANUEL LITRAN FOR PARIS MATCH

OPPOSITE: A DETAIL OF THE LESAGE EMBROIDERY UPON THE WILLIAMVINTAGE BALMAIN HAUTE-COUTURE BALLGOWN, c1954

While Dior was taking the world by storm following his New Look of 1947, he was also diversifying his market. Establishing Dior New York in 1948 and ensuring that diffusion lines of his haute couture were available as quickly as possible, Dior sought unprecedented global domination and brand awareness. Balmain, however, chose to focus upon the vastly wealthy women who came to Paris for the finest haute couture. In 1961 American journalist Nadeane Walker wrote a vituperative review of Balmain's latest offering and recounted his description of his average client: 'She's rich and not one of the new rich ... she plays at wrapping herself in what could have been the blanket of her grandmother's coachman'. She concludes, 'He makes it clear that he sews only for the lilies of the field, who toil not.'

While the dress is emblematic of the house of Balmain at its height, it is also a lesson in the incredible skills of Maison Lesage, the Parisian embroidery house still in existence and acquired by Chanel in 2002. When François Lesage, son of the company's founder Albert, was awarded the Maître d'Art by the French Ministry of Culture in 2011, the Minister said, 'I cannot

Photo KUBLIN

imagine haute couture without embroidery, nor embroidery without Monsieur Lesage'. The work of Lesage is undisputedly the greatest of all Parisian embroiderers, but during the twentieth century there were more than fifty similar houses, all of which carried out the finest work for the couture ateliers.

Maison Lesage, alongside other houses including Maison Rebe, Maison Vermont and Maison Brossin de Mere, worked with crystal cut by Swarovski, buttons made by Mesrine, feather trims formed by Lemarié and untold other artisanal companies, whose sole purpose was to add another layer of luxury and three-dimensionality to Parisian haute couture. It is only when realising that each of these companies worked for nearly all the great couturiers and that the structure of these smaller companies was at times far more complex than the couture houses themselves, that the artistic signatures, personalities and chaos of industry during the golden age comes alive. Just as Balmain chose Lesage for the embroidery of this dress, Lesage would, in turn, have chosen Swarovski for the finest hand-cut crystals and an artisan anywhere – from a village in the Hautes-Pyrénées to a city in Lorraine – for the silver and thread work. Each facet of the couture industry would feed another and for the finest work on haute couture a house may have used an ageing woman in an outlying town who had learnt her unique skills from generations before her.

During a stay on the Greek island of Mykonos, as I was discussing my vocation with a local tailor, he disappeared into the minuscule, whitewashed fisherman's cottage behind him and emerged with a yellowing letter handwritten by Christian Dior. Never before documented, Dior too had holidayed on Mykonos in 1953 and had been so impressed by the fine cotton offerings of the tailor's grandfather that he had the undershirts for his acclaimed couture collection made by the seventy-year-old former fisherman. Afterwards Dior had written to thank him for the 'chemises superbes'. This spectacular ball gown is not only a shining example of Parisian haute couture, but also the culmination of all of the houses, companies, personalities, obsessions and labours uniting to create one, unforgettable moment for the woman who would be lucky enough to slip inside it and for whom, at that moment, 'life was exciting again'.

OPPOSITE: AN ADVERTISEMENT FOR THE BALMAIN AND LESAGE COLLECTION OF 1954, PHOTOGRAPHED FOR L'OFFICIEL

The Balmain Legacy

Romona Keveza

Dior

Dior

12

Dessès

13

and the
Egyptian Influence

There are few designers in the world who have had as great an impact upon contemporary fashion as JEAN DESSÈS, yet his name and triumphs are largely unknown.

The creator of a sartorial language as recognisable and as relevant as Dior's New Look, Dessès has influenced, amongst countless other designers, Halston, Christian Lacroix, Gianni Versace, Giorgio Armani and, most notably, his former protégé Valentino Garavani. This 1953 haute-couture dress, in scarlet-red silk chiffon, contains within it clues to the ancient past that so inspired Dessès as a designer.

While Christian Dior was inspired by grand European portraiture of the eighteenth and nineteenth centuries, and Madame Grès by the grace of Hellenic sculpture, their contemporary Jean Dessès could not help but be inspired by the legendary city in which he was born, Alexandria. Founded by Macedonian Emperor Alexander the Great in 331BC, Alexandria was part of an empire that stretched from Greece to the Indian subcontinent. Dessès, born in 1904 to wealthy Greeks living in Egypt, had an extraordinary duality, growing up as the resident of an African city that was as saturated in the glory of Classical Greece and the myths of the Gods as it was in the glory of Ancient Egypt and the art of the Pharaohs.

Dessès was expected by his family to become a diplomat and, having obtained a degree in law in Alexandria, he relocated to Paris to continue his studies at the age of twenty-one. His life changed, however, when a Parisian couturier, who had been shown his personal fashion sketches by a mutual friend, convinced the young Dessès to abandon a career in the diplomatic corps for one in the world of Parisian haute couture. After tenure within her house, where he absorbed the technical and artistic requirements of a fashion house, Dessès resigned and established his own atelier in 1936 with the backing of his family money. Opening to great acclaim, it was first reviewed in French *Vogue* in 1937 and Dessès soon found favour amongst the social elite.

TOP: A STATUE OF THE GODDESS SELKET FROM THE TOMB OF TUT ANKH AMUN, c1370BC

MIDDLE: A STATUE OF NEFERTITI, c1365BC

BELOW: THE THRONE OF TUT ANKH AMUN, c1370BC

OPPOSITE: A WILLIAMVINTAGE JEAN DESSÈS HAUTE-COUTURE DRESS IN CYCLAMEN-PINK SILK CHIFFON, c1953

While the duality of Dessès's birthplace enhanced his success with international clients, European and American press coverage at the time contained a barely repressed xenophobia. In 1947, the year of Dior's revolutionary New Look, Ruth Millett reviewed Dessès's Autumn/Winter collection under the banner 'Longer Dresses and Broader Beams' and noted that 'Jean Dessès, a round-faced little Egyptian-born Greek who draped bits of the Orient into his new fashions ... is reported to be the principal builder of clothes to the Egyptian Royal household'. Despite the patronising description of Dessès and the rather underwhelming reviews of his daywear, within a few years his royal clients had increased in number. Princess Margaret, the Duchess of Windsor and Queen Frederika of Greece all became devotees of his designs and vital to his commercial success, Dessès also found favour with the women of the Greek shipping dynasties. In perhaps the most exuberant display of one-upmanship ever seen within the fashion world, Aristotle Onassis, knowing that his business rival Stavros Niarchos's wife adored Jean Dessès, decided to 'buy' the house of Dessès for his own wife Tina, who also happened to be the sister of Niarchos's wife.

As Dessès's client list became increasingly stellar and the ownership of one of his dresses – as indeed the ownership of the house itself – became seen as a trophy, his designs became more and more exuberant. From the muted palette of his pre-war years and the subdued colours that reflected both rationing and the mood of wartime oppression, Dessès came into his own in the joyous years of the 1950s, which have become known as the 'golden age of haute couture'. Confections in chiffon and silk were offered in the brightest of reds, blues, greens and yellows, and it was Dessès's selection of vibrant colours that first references an Egyptian influence; the ancient Egyptian pigments of chrysocolla green, ochre red and 'Alexandria' blue, the first synthetic colour invented in Egypt in 2500BC, were all represented within the couture house.

Just as the colour palette chosen by Dessès became increasingly Egyptian in approach, so too did his design ethos. While there is a strong element of Hellenic design within a Jean Dessès dress, it is vital to remember that in addition to the influence of his Greek parentage, his clients included both the Greek royal family and the extraordinarily wealthy Livanos, Niarchos and Onassis dynasties, who were supplied by his secondary couture atelier, opened in Athens in 1955; a number of Dessès's designs from this period are more re-creations of Hellenic costume than contemporary designs. However, the signature of nearly every Jean Dessès evening dress is not the drapery, all too often assigned to his Greek roots, but the knife-sharp pleating to the bodice, as seen within this dress, which speaks of a far more archaic source.

OPPOSITE: A JEAN DESSÈS HAUTE-COUTURE DRESS, PHOTOGRAPHED BY PHILIPPE POTTIER FOR L'OFFICIEL, 1952

The Dessès Legacy

Ralph & Russo   *Dior*   *Elie Saab*

A WILLIAMVINTAGE JEAN DESSÈS HAUTE-
COUTURE DRESS IN TEAL BLUE SILK, c1956

While Madame Grès was garnering favour with her intensely classicising couture in fine silk jersey, draped, rolled and folded in homage to the sculptors of ancient Greece, Dessès chose to work in silk chiffon, which could be pressed to a razor's edge to achieve an effect clearly inspired by the graphic, linear designs seen in early Egyptian dynastic art. Even in silk, an haute-couture dress by Dessès holds this far more ancient language. The extraordinary 1958 silk ball gown shown on the previous pages contains a drapery that, upon closer inspection, is far more reminiscent of the stylised palm and iris decoration featured in Egyptian painting, sculpture and metalwork as it is of classical Greek statuary.

When I discover a Jean Dessès dress, I feast my eyes upon its rich jewel tones and ancient inspirations and cannot help but think of an event that took place in Luxor in 1923 and which must have had huge impact upon the nineteen-year-old Jean Dessès, who was still a resident of Egypt at the time. Having spent years excavating the Valley of the Kings, the English archaeologist and Egyptologist Howard Carter had, with one tap of a chisel, opened up a doorway that had been sealed for more than 3,500 years. The 'Boy King' Tut Ankh Amun had been discovered and news of his solid gold coffin, perfectly preserved golden throne and the countless artistic riches contained within his tomb set the world aflame.

On every wall, on the surface of his coffin and on the back of his throne are renditions of the kings and queens of Egypt, each shown wearing crisp, linear robes all too similar to the dresses Dessès would go on to create.

The house of Jean Dessès foundered within the shifting, youth-focused decade of the 1960s and, having closed its haute-couture business in 1960, it closed its prêt-à-porter operation and its doors forever in 1965. The relic of a different time, it lay forgotten for more than thirty years, a distant memory of only fashion historians and designers. However, the extraordinary colours and unique designs would resurface in an age of colour photography, at the dawn of the new millennium. In 1999 Naomi Campbell wore a vintage haute-couture dress by Jean Dessès to a Christie's party, and slowly interest in the house increased. His work was chosen again in 2001 by Renée Zellweger for the Oscars, in 2004 by Kate Moss and in 2006 by Jennifer Lopez. The ravishing haute couture of Jean Dessès and his extraordinary, multicultural and inspirational designs have become as treasured today as they were when they were first created by the 'round-faced, little Egyptian-born Greek'.

OPPOSITE: A JEAN DESSÈS DRESS, PHOTOGRAPHED BY GEORGES SAAD FOR L'OFFICIEL, 1952

The Dessès Legacy

Giorgio Armani

Ralph & Russo

Saint Laurent

The Boy King of Dior

When Dior's twenty-one-year-old assistant YVES SAINT LAURENT was named as his successor, it led to some of the greatest changes in haute couture ever witnessed.

On 23rd October 1957 the unthinkable happened and the fashion world was plunged into mourning and deep confusion. Christian Dior, the man at the helm of the largest and most influential fashion house in the world and believed by many to have single-handedly revived Parisian haute couture, was gone forever. Dior had died from a heart attack at only fifty-two years of age. The empire he left behind included haute couture, ready-to-wear, perfume and accessories sold in over twenty countries with an annual income in excess of twenty-million dollars.

While over 2,500 mourners attended the funeral, the question on everybody's mind was who could possibly replace Monsieur Dior? For the owner of Dior, Marcel Boussac, such was the loss that for a time he considered closing the house. Instead, he followed the advice of Dior himself who had named his successor prior to his death. It was an extraordinary choice. Christian Dior had decided that the heir apparent of his empire was his young, unknown assistant. The decision ushered in one of the more explosive periods in the history of the house and resulted in a volatile and damaging relationship between Boussac and the house's fledgling Creative Director. Ultimately, the appointment led to creation of another couture house that would become as legendary and powerful as that of Dior. The name of Dior's young assistant, and now successor, was Yves Saint Laurent; twenty-one years old and the new 'Boy King' of Dior.

Born in French Algeria in 1936, Yves Saint Laurent was the child of wealthy and privileged parents who understood and supported their rather awkward, insular and artistic son. From an early age, Saint Laurent would advise his mother on her wardrobe and spend his free time sketching costume

TOP: THE COVER OF PARIS MATCH *MOURNING THE DEATH OF DIOR, 1957*

CENTRE: THE DIOR MIDINETTES *READ OF THE DEATH OF CHRISTIAN DIOR, OCTOBER 1957*

RIGHT: A YOUNG SAINT LAURENT POSES WITH ONE OF HIS DESIGNS, 1954

OPPOSITE: A WILLIAMVINTAGE DIOR HAUTE-COUTURE SUIT IN IVORY AND BLACK WOOL BOUCLÉ, AUTUMN/WINTER 1959

designs for the plays that he would enact with his siblings. By the time he reached his teenage years, it was clear that all the young Yves wanted to do was to create fashion. Through his family connections, he was introduced to the Editor-in-Chief of French *Vogue*, Michel de Brunhoff, who was deeply impressed by the quiet but assured young man. When Saint Laurent had completed his studies at the École de la Chambre Syndicale de la Couture, de Brunhoff introduced the precocious eighteen-year-old to Christian Dior after seeing a few of Saint Laurent's sketches. The green Saint Laurent and the great Dior had both been working on similar ideas and on conclusion of the meeting Dior hired Saint Laurent on the spot.

While Saint Laurent was initially employed on relatively mundane tasks, including the decoration of the Dior boutique and the design of a few accessories, his talent and determination was obvious. He soon rose within the empire to become the only assistant Dior ever employed and Dior became confident enough in Saint Laurent to allow him to contribute haute-couture designs of his own. The first dress known to be by Saint Laurent for the house of Dior was immortalised by Richard Avedon in his 1955 photograph *Dovima with the Elephants*, which shows a restrained but dynamic design. Saint Laurent was only nineteen-years-old at the time, yet his work already bore the label of Dior haute couture, had been photographed on Dior's favourite model and had been captured by one of the greatest fashion photographers of the day. By the Autumn/Winter collection of 1957, the final collection by Monsieur Dior, Saint Laurent had contributed thirty-five haute-couture dress designs.

Following the death of Dior, Saint Laurent's first collection as Creative Director in Spring 1958 was credited with saving the Dior empire. His 'Trapeze' collection was lauded by the fashion press, adored by the existing clients of Monsieur Dior and spoke a language that also appealed to more youthful women, who appreciated his flowing lines and changed silhouette. However, his subsequent Autumn/Winter collection, while loved by the younger clientele, did not find favour with the all-important older demographic. The six collections designed by Saint Laurent at Dior were alternately praised and lambasted. The collections of both 1959 and 1960 polarised opinion, infuriated Marcel Boussac and led not only to Saint Laurent's departure from Dior but also, ultimately, to his internment in a mental institution.

While Saint Laurent entirely understood the vision of Dior, the man that he always referred to as 'My Master, and my only Master', Saint Laurent refused to become merely a phantom at the helm. Instead he decided to develop the house in line with his own ideas and what he saw as the future of fashion and haute couture. Already being warned that his modernising design ethic was closer to that of Chanel than of Dior, this suit by Saint Laurent from the Dior Autumn/Winter 1959 couture collection is perhaps the closest that the two houses ever came to one another. One of the final nails in the coffin for Saint Laurent at Dior, despite being one of the most exquisite suits ever created, it is constructed in fine ivory bouclé, trimmed with black bouclé and lined in ivory silk. The dress is accompanied by a cardigan-style jacket and, while the design has all the hallmarks of Dior with its nipped-in waist and darted tulip skirt, it is undeniably influenced by post-war Chanel. Daringly short, daringly fitted and daringly similar in design to Dior's great rival, it is an example of two designers speaking in resounding union. Looking at this suit, it is no great surprise that the only designer Chanel ever suggested as the successor to her empire was Yves Saint Laurent.

One can only empathise with the young Saint Laurent in the final year of the fifties. Impossibly young and possessing both extraordinary talent and vision, he seemed to already understand the woman of the impending sixties, yet his employer and the house that he represented would forever be in the shadow of Monsieur Dior and his 'New Look' of 1947. This haute-couture dress by Yves Saint Laurent is also from the Dior Autumn/Winter 1959 collection and was christened 'Zenaide'. Constructed from deep-green silk set upon silk georgette and lined in caramel silk organza, the dress is a superb example of Saint Laurent's understanding of all the principles of Christian Dior and his ability to reinterpret them to his own taste. The dress is a mesmerising sheath of spiralling, ruched silk, caressing every curve of the wearer's body. Celebrating a new fluidity, the dress has neither the internal corset nor constraining boning associated with a Dior cocktail dress of this period. Internally weighted to ensure the dress not only hangs perfectly but sways just enough to fully celebrate the notion of 'the wiggle', it illustrates perfectly the growing sensuality within the more daring late fifties. The Zenaide, despite its origins within a cooly received collection, has become one of the most iconic dresses of the twentieth century.

After the disappointing and commercially unsuccessful Autumn/Winter 1959 collection, Saint Laurent designed a safer and more mundane collection for Spring 1960 under direct orders from his employer, Boussac. However, he was not to be constrained for long. His Autumn/Winter 1960

OPPOSITE; THE MODEL SUZY PARKER POSES WITH YVES SAINT LAURENT, PHOTOGRAPHED BY RICHARD AVEDON, 1959

A WILLIAMVINTAGE DIOR HAUTE-
COUTURE 'ZENAIDE' DRESS IN DEEP
GREEN SILK, AUTUMN/WINTER 1959

collection, known as the 'Beat' collection, showcased pea coats, shift dresses and what Saint Laurent saw on the streets of Paris, London and New York. Marcel Boussac was incensed. The Dior client was outraged at such a revolutionary departure from the house lines and language. Fearing a huge drop in sales, Boussac took drastic action. Having ensured that Saint Laurent had been excused compulsory military service for the previous two years, in 1960 Boussac allowed his conscription, effectively removing Saint Laurent from not only the house of Dior but also from France. A matter of weeks after being sent to Algeria, Saint Laurent was hospitalised due to emotional trauma as a result of merciless hazing by his fellow conscripts. He was returned to France a shadow of the man he once was. While under sedation and enduring electro-shock therapy in Val-de-Grâce, a sanatorium in Paris, he heard the news that he had been fired from Dior and replaced by Marc Bohan, who had been working on the Dior London collections since 1958. Bohan was a more commercially friendly designer, who went on to rule the house of Dior for a further twenty-nine years.

Disgraced by his dismissal and with his confidence shattered, at only twenty-four years old Yves Saint Laurent was considered by many to be redundant in every way; his dismissal from Dior seen as a judgement more than a corporate decision. However, few people fully understood the dynamic between Saint Laurent and his lover, Pierre Bergé. A forceful, commercially aware man who understood Saint Laurent's brilliance and his frailty, Bergé, nursed him back to health, took legal advice and started discreet discussions with wealthy American industrialists interested in investing in the career of the former Boy King of Dior. In 1961 a resurgent Saint Laurent made two announcements. The first was that he had won a claim against Dior for his dismissal and had been paid substantial damages. The second was that with these damages and the investment of J Mack Robinson, a wealthy American financier, he would be establishing his own couture house. The time of Saint Laurent as understudy had ended and the era of Saint Laurent the couturier was about to begin.

OPPOSITE: THE DIOR HAUTE-COUTURE 'ZENAIDE' PHOTOGRAPHED BY IRVING PENN FOR AMERICAN VOGUE, SEPTEMBER 1959

The Saint Laurent Legacy

Marchesa

Moschino

Marchesa

Givenchy

The Count and his Princesses

Having launched his house – now one of the largest in the world – aged only twenty-five, HUBERT DE GIVENCHY has outlived all of his contemporaries from the golden age of couture.

Givenchy and his role in fashion can be best understood from the simplest of conversations. At a formal lunch in 1961, the host turned to his female guest and asked, 'Is that a Givenchy you are wearing?' The reply, 'Why how clever of you, however did you know?', was met with 'I'm getting pretty good at it now that fashion is becoming more important than politics'. The lunch in question was being held at the White House, the genial host was President John F Kennedy and the female guest was Princess Grace of Monaco, formerly the American movie star Grace Kelly. Givenchy's designs were being recognised by presidents and worn by princesses and in the 1960s being a princess had never been quite so cool and notions of royalty never quite so broad.

The man who founded what has become one of the largest fashion houses in the world was born into the privileged French aristocracy with the full name Count Hubert James Taffin de Givenchy, the son of the Marquis Lucien Taffin de Givenchy. Described by *Vogue* in 1966 as 'Six feet six inches tall and handsomer than almost any movie star', he was, without doubt, one of the best-looking men of his generation and equally one of the best-dressed. Photographs of Givenchy from the 1950s to the present day show a man comfortable within his own skin, effortlessly elegant and patrician, and it is this easy, aristocratic demeanour that suffuses not only the man, but also his legendary designs.

This haute-couture evening dress from 1963 is a superb example of the house in full stride. Constructed of the palest blue silk shot through with silver thread, the dress glistens like ice, while its seemingly simple lines conceal

TOP: AUDREY HEPBURN WEARING GIVENCHY WHEN COLLECTING HER ACADEMY AWARD FOR ROMAN HOLIDAY, 1954

CENTRE: FIRST LADY OF THE UNITED STATES OF AMERICA JACQUELINE KENNEDY WEARING GIVENCHY AT THE PALACE OF VERSAILLES, 1961

LEFT: PRINCESS GRACE OF MONACO WEARING GIVENCHY AT THE WEDDING OF PRINCE JUAN CARLOS OF SPAIN, 1962

OPPOSITE: A WILLIAMVINTAGE GIVENCHY HAUTE-COUTURE DRESS IN BLUE AND SILVER SILK BROCADE, c1963

extraordinary technical expertise. Underneath the silk, the dress has twelve equally placed bands of crinoline to keep the perfect bell shape of the dress in place when worn. Each of the seven panels of silk from which the dress is formed is shaped to create a sinuous, flowing curve from the arch of a shoulder blade to the curve of a hip bone before terminating in a full skirt. As with many of Givenchy's designs from this period, its austerity of design shows the impact upon Givenchy of another great couturier, Cristóbal Balenciaga.

As a teenager passionate about fashion and initially desirous of a position at the house of Balenciaga, Givenchy had been turned away by Balenciaga's stern Directrice, who would not grant him an appointment. Despondent, the young Givenchy found employment at the couture house of Jacques Fath through family connections before subsequent positions with Robert Piguet, Lucien Lelong and finally a four-year employment at the couture house of the ebullient Elsa Schiaparelli. By now highly trained, with a superb working knowledge of the couture industry, and having seen his fellow employees at Lelong, Pierre Balmain and Christian Dior launch their own houses, he followed suit and in 1952 the house of Givenchy was born.

ABOVE: PRINCESS LEE RADZIWILL AND HER SISTER, FIRST LADY OF THE UNITED STATES OF AMERICA JACQUELINE KENNEDY, BOTH WEARING GIVENCHY, 1965

OPPOSITE: AUDREY HEPBURN WEARING GIVENCHY, PHOTOGRAPHED BY BERT STERN FOR AMERICAN VOGUE, APRIL 1963

Givenchy met Balenciaga the following year and the two men went on to have a lifelong friendship. The older Balenciaga became a mentor to the young aristocrat with whom he shared an almost identical sense of luxury and belief in how a woman should dress. When questioned about his mentor in 1973 Givenchy said: 'Mr Balenciaga combined creative genius, a flair for the avant-garde and a technique that has remained unsurpassed. He was the complete creator.'

With both men holding their shows later than every other designer, barring many established and respected members of the press and exhibiting an increasing similarity in design ethic, an air of secrecy was created. American fashion columnist Eugenia Sheppard, writing for the *Herald Tribune* in 1959, reported that 'Secret operatives filed through the underground tunnel that is said to connect Balenciaga and Givenchy salons, now across the street from each other.'

There was, of course, no tunnel, but such was the relationship between the two designers that there may as well have been one built.

No discussion of Givenchy can be had without reference to the woman who would become both one of his greatest friends and his muse, the British actress Audrey Hepburn. Having first met in 1953 for Hepburn's wardrobe in *Sabrina* (1954), they went on to work together on many of her greatest movies, including *Funny Face* (1957), *Breakfast at Tiffany's* (1961), *Charade* (1963), *When it Sizzles* (1964) and *How to Steal a Million* (1966). Symbiotic from the start, the relationship helped shape both their destinies and *Vogue* summed it up as follows: 'What fires his imagination races hers. The message he cuts into cloth she beams into the world with the special wit and stylishness of a great star.' At the time this dress was designed, Givenchy and Hepburn were creating a language based not upon the rise of street fashion, modernism or the Space Race, but towards an ideal of transcendent style. Working together for more than forty years and both iconic figures to this day, they succeeded.

If the relationship between Givenchy and Hepburn were to be reduced to one dress, it must be the black sheath worn by Hepburn in *Breakfast at Tiffany's*. Luxurious, elongating and chic, the dress has become the benchmark for elegance for over fifty years and a hallmark of both Givenchy and Hepburn. When last sold at auction in 2006, the dress achieved the unimaginable sum of £467,000.

While the relationship between Givenchy and Hepburn is perhaps the most documented, Givenchy's clients were an extraordinary group of women, including Jacqueline Kennedy and her sister Princess Lee Radziwill, the Duchess of Windsor, Princess Salimah Aga Khan, Empress Farah Pahlavi, Princess Grace of Monaco, Marlene Dietrich, Deborah Kerr, Lauren Bacall, Ingrid Bergman, Diana Vreeland and Maria Callas. A picture emerges of the Givenchy woman; exquisite, impeccable, timeless and in many ways untouchable and imperial, they are all members of a ruling class, whether monarchical, political or creative. This 1963 haute-couture gown by Hubert de Givenchy has within it one other key feature: given Givenchy's stellar client list of the great and the good, its distinctive, panelled, A-line silhouette is an invention of Givenchy's christened the 'Princess Cut'.

OPPOSITE: AUDREY HEPBURN WEARING GIVENCHY HAUTE COUTURE, PHOTOGRAPHED BY WILLIAM KLEIN FOR AMERICAN VOGUE, *OCTOBER 1966*

The Givenchy Legacy

Zac Posen

Chanel

Dior

Chanel

After the
Third Reich

From its restrained launch in 1954 to its present-day incarnation, a CHANEL suit has remained a beacon of luxury and stealth chic for more than fifty years.

When thinking of Chanel it is more often the iconic, tailored suit that enters our mind rather than the earlier glories of a fashion house that was first mentioned in *Vogue* in 1913. To understand the impact of the Chanel suit, it is vital to remember the dark period of Chanel's life and career that surrounded its birth and led her to fall from being a source of national pride to becoming the most hated woman in France.

This 1967 haute-couture suit of ivory wool bouclé, trimmed in black braid, lined in ivory silk and set with gilt buttons is the *sine qua non* of the Chanel suit. The byword for restrained elegance, a version of this suit was owned by the most fabled style icon of the day, Grace Kelly. Having had a glorious Hollywood career before completing the fairytale of falling in love with a dashing European royal, with her icy beauty and royal status, Princess Grace was the ultimate Chanel client. It is extraordinary to think that the house could have crumbled on the day the first true Chanel suit was launched.

After her glories and triumphs throughout the 1910s, 1920s and 1930s, with her impeccable couture creations and Chanel Number 5 becoming the world's bestselling fragrance, Gabrielle Chanel was an immensely wealthy woman and a respected global figure. While she had always faced gossip about her many lovers and patrons, nebulous sexuality and use of recreational drugs, it was all rather harmless and best summed up in her own words: 'I don't care what you think of me, I do not think about you at all.' However, the events of 1939 and her actions thereafter took Chanel from being a subject of interest to the *beau monde* of Paris to a subject of interest to British and French Intelligence agencies, and with good reason.

At the outbreak of the Second World War the house of Chanel employed nearly four-thousand women; this vast workforce was a vital part of the French economy. Upon confirmation that France was being invaded by Germany and despite the pleadings of both the French government and the Chambre Syndicale de la Haute Couture, Chanel chose to close her factories, workshops and couture house, sack her entire workforce with immediate and devastating effect, and leave Paris. It was a terrific blow not just to the economy but to France as a whole, seeing 'Coco' flee Paris.

TOP: CHANEL HAUTE COUTURE ON THE STREETS, PHOTOGRAPHED BY PAUL SCHÜTZE, 1960

CENTRE: THE CHANEL FRONT ROW WITH BARBRA STREISAND, ELSA MARTINELLI AND MARLENE DIETRICH, PHOTOGRAPHED BY BILL EPPRIDGE, 1966

BOTTOM: CHANEL HAUTE COUTURE ON THE STREETS, PHOTOGRAPHED BY PAUL SCHÜTZE, 1960

OPPOSITE: A WILLIAMVINTAGE CHANEL HAUTE-COUTURE SUIT IN IVORY BOUCLÉ, 1967

Paris fell to the Germans in July 1940 and it is what Chanel chose to do when she came back to the occupied city that tainted her reputation forever; she returned to the rue Cambon and her suite in the Ritz Hotel and entered into an affair with the German aristocrat and Nazi officer, Baron Hans Günther von Dincklage. Handsome, titled and a mere forty-four years old when Chanel was fifty-eight, his role might have been yet another dominant, blue-blooded lover, after relationships with Étienne Balsan, 'Boy' Capel, Grand Duke Dmitri Pavlovich of Russia and the Duke of Westminster. For von Dincklage, however, there was likely an ulterior motive to the relationship, which has been the subject of debate for more than half a century: the recruitment of Chanel as a Nazi collaborator.

There are countless contemporary statements regarding Chanel's role, but she exacerbated the situation when she met with Nazi Spymaster Walter Schellenberg and became a part of the Nazi 'Operation Modelhut' with her codename 'Westminster'. Depending on reports, the operation was either a plan to coax Britain into passive submission or to inform Churchill that there were senior Nazi officials who had misgivings over the actions of the Führer. However, Vera Lombardi, Chanel's long-term friend and companion on the operation, arrived at the British Embassy in Madrid denouncing Gabrielle Chanel and her travelling party as Nazi spies.

Following the liberation of Paris in 1944, Chanel faced enquiries under the Épuration légale to either determine her guilt as a collaborator or to testify regarding the potential guilt of her associates, and she also faced numerous dealings with British Intelligence. Given Chanel's close friendships with the Duke of Westminster, the Duke and Duchess of Windsor, Prime Minister Churchill and members of the British royal family and Parliament who were reputed to have anti-Semitic tendencies, her response when asked how she avoided charges of collaboration was of great interest. Chanel's famed comment, 'Churchill freed me', has a deeper context as many believe Chanel was spared to avoid a court case that would have been highly embarrassing for many international parties. Chanel clearly held Schellenberg in high regard; after his early release due to ill health from a prison sentence imposed at the Nuremberg Trials, it was Chanel who paid his expenses. When Schellenberg died in 1952, eighteen months before the house of Chanel reopened its doors, she paid for his funeral. An interview from September 1944 between Chanel and MI6 agent Malcolm Muggeridge gives the best indication as to how Chanel justified her actions; when asked directly whose

OPPOSITE: PRINCESS GRACE OF MONACO, FORMERLY THE FILM STAR GRACE KELLY, IN HER CHANEL HAUTE-COUTURE SUIT, 1967

The Chanel Legacy

Moschino

Cynthia Rowley

Moschino

*A WILLIAMVINTAGE CHANEL HAUTE-COUTURE
SEVEN-PIECE ENSEMBLE, INCLUDING BRACES,
CRAVAT AND PEAKED CAP, 1968*

ABOVE: A MODEL WEARING AN CHANEL HAUTE-
COUTURE SUIT WITHIN THE CHANEL ATELIER, 1972

side she was on in the war, her response was, 'On neither side, of course. I stood up for myself as I have always done'.

By the 1950s fashion had changed enormously since Chanel closed the doors of her haute-couture atelier in 1939. The dominance of female couturiers had passed and her contemporaries, Madeleine Vionnet, Jeanne Lanvin and Elsa Schiaparelli, were in second position to Dior, the new King of Haute Couture, and his court of designer disciples. While Chanel despised all that Dior stood for and referred to his dresses as 'boned horrors', his approach of placing women in corsets and bustles was adopted by Fath, Balmain, Balenciaga and many others. Chanel was incensed that after decades of work ensuring women were able to wear clothes that enhanced their life, their freedom and their natural form, Dior was placing women back on a pedestal to be treated as objects of worship.

In 1954, after fifteen years, the house of Chanel reopened its doors and re-entered the world of haute couture. At its helm was Chanel, a sixty-eight-year-old woman tarnished by her private life and with the French and European press ready to pour scorn upon her. Her first collection debuted and, by all reports, Chanel had not moved on from her 1930s heyday. Sedate models on the runway, loose-fitting clothes and Art Deco silhouettes that were neither part of the haute-couture New Look nor different enough to put Chanel back on her

throne were met with a resounding silence. Bettina Ballard, the Fashion Director of American *Vogue* and a highly influential figure in fashion, had already agreed with Chanel to cover her return to fashion and selected a few garments from the show both for her own wardrobe and for a photographic shoot. One item chosen by Ballard was a simple navy wool suit ensemble, of skirt, jacket, crisp white shirt with necktie and a matching hat. It was this suit, luckily chosen by Bettina and later photographed for *Vogue*, that saved the house of Chanel.

At a time when Paris was obsessed with the New Look and women were placed within their clothes, rather than clothe themselves, Chanel's reinterpretation of her previous designs and her sharp eye for comfortable, chic tailoring proved hugely popular with American and British buyers. Within a year Chanel was gracing the covers of *Vogue* and *Elle* magazines once more, and her coterie of aristocratic young models and ambassadors were out in force wearing the latest Chanel creations. Coco was back, her empire rebuilt, her fortune increasing and her seemingly simple suit desired by wealthy women everywhere. The Chanel suit was seen in jersey, wool gabardine, tweed and wool bouclé, and the Chanel obsession for tailoring was evident throughout. Sharply executed shoulders and a sleeve line that barely wrinkled when the arm was folded, jackets weighted by gold chains in order to hold their shape and shirts that were secured within the skirts by a series of buttons all ensured that, once put on, the Chanel woman would remain impeccable. A symbol of discreet yet immense wealth and cultured elegance, the Chanel suit had a strength Dior overlooked. It was something a woman could put on herself and walk, drive and live in; it became the original power suit and remains the template for modern tailoring.

A defining quality of the Chanel couture house was the way in which the Chanel identity was woven through every collection. Whether worked in Edwardian jerseys, 1920s chiffon, 1930s lace or other fabrics and decades, it is impossible to miss the extraordinary execution and sensibility in her garments. The evolution of the Chanel suit seemed organic and slow, but from its austere, subtle launch in 1954 to the ivory and gilt version of 1967, there was a change of pace and style, further evident in this haute-couture ensemble of 1968. Comprised of seven pieces, the suit is extraordinary not only for surviving intact, but for showing Chanel's understanding of women's changing taste.

Chanel was eighty-five when she designed this spectacularly hip, androgynous suit, ensuring that her house remained at the pinnacle of haute couture in the chaotic, libertarian 1960s. It must have amused Chanel who forty years previously had introduced trousers, cravats and influences of men's tailoring to see the wave of 'fashion revolutionaries' adopt and adapt so many of her signatures into their designs in the name of modernity. Constructed from waxed cotton, this suit was designed as part of an ensemble that included skirt, jacket, shirt, braces, peaked cap, hat pin and cravat. While its components are identical to her original suit from some fifteen years earlier, the language has advanced. By this time Chanel's love of the masculine/feminine had been noted and developed by Yves Saint Laurent, with his 'Le Smoking' collection, and Rudi Gernreich, with his erotic play on the subject in an aesthetic that was a fusion of 1960s Americana and 1930s Weimar cabaret. The Chanel obsession with sharp tailoring was developed by Courrèges, Ungaro and a host of designers whom Chanel loathed, despite working to the same goals: the empowerment and freeing of women in fashion.

The house of Chanel has been at the forefront of haute couture for over a century, but the legend of Chanel the woman remains indistinct, a complex amalgam of brutalism and romanticism, survivalism and sacrifice, brilliance and naivety, but above all the legend of a woman who knew herself and never apologised for her beliefs. As Chanel said, 'The most courageous act for a woman is to think for yourself. Aloud.'

The Chanel Legacy

Vivienne Westwood   *Moschino*   *Henry Holland*

Courrèges

The Journey to the Moon

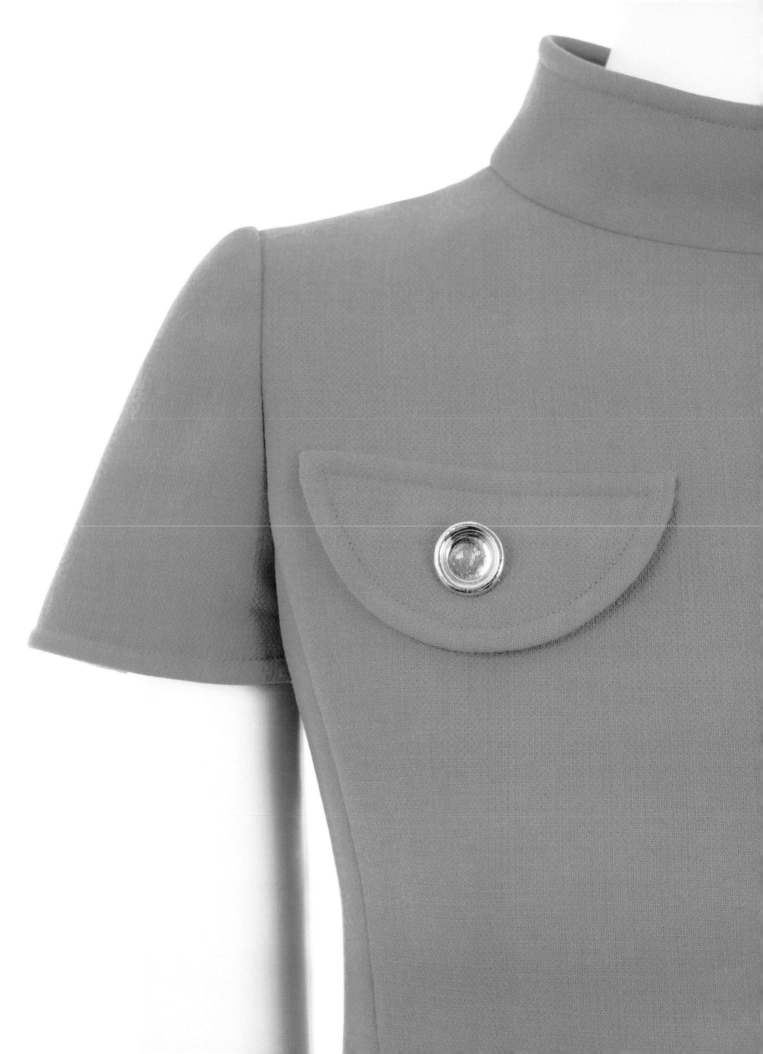

The embodiment of the hopes and dreams of a generation, an ANDRÉ COURRÈGES dress is about the dawn of a new age and the thrill of the unknown.

TOP: A BRUSHED-STEEL WATER TOWER BY EERO SAARINEN, PHOTOGRAPHED BY BALTHAZAR KORAB, 1962

ABOVE: THE JOHN F KENNEDY TWA TERMINAL, NEW YORK CITY, PHOTOGRAPHED BY BALTHAZAR KORAB, 1962

OPPOSITE: A WILLIAMVINTAGE COURRÈGES DRESS IN GREEN WOOL, c1965

A Courrèges dress is about far more than crisp tailoring, clean lines and the go-go girls of the 1960s. It symbolised the aspirations of a modern, liberal generation of women who no longer wanted to look back to a pre-war heyday. Just as Dior had changed the face of fashion and the silhouette of women in the 1940s, so too did Courrèges in the 1960s. However there lies an abyss between the inspirations of the two men. Whereas Dior and his New Look of 1947 had put women back into corsets and swathes of fabric, an approach to dressing last seen in eighteenth-century France, Courrèges chose not to re-create a version of the past but to imagine a bold new future.

When thinking of the 1960s and the dawn of popular culture it is all too easy to separate fashion, film, literature and architecture, when in fact they had one common theme for nearly a decade, the Space Age. First ignited by Russia's launch of Sputnik 1 in 1957 and culminating in the moon landing of America's Apollo 11 in 1969, the 1960s was a decade obsessed by the future, and by both the scientific and humanist ideologies brought about by notions of space travel and the Space Race.

A Courrèges dress may now seem familiar and not necessarily extraordinary to our eyes. The reason for this is not that the dress has been rendered obsolete in the fifty years since it was designed, but rather because during that time it has become the foundation for fashion design in the twenty-first century. Constructed of bright-green gabardine, this dress is an iconic example of André Courrèges at his apex in the mid-1960s and contains within it nearly every hallmark associated with his extraordinary designs: its pronounced A-line silhouette, exposed welt seams, faux pockets, sparse decoration and use of solid, bold colour.

After a decade spent under the tutelage of the great couturier Cristóbal Balenciaga, Courrèges established his own house in 1961, and while his *raison d'être* was to create clothing for the modern woman, both his time at the grand couture house and his formal education were cornerstones of his success. Having initially trained as a civil engineer, Courrèges's passion for understanding the construction, form

and function of objects was allowed to blossom during his tenure with Balenciaga. Referred to as 'The Master' by Givenchy, Balenciaga was a couturier known for his extraordinary technical abilities and almost magical understanding of fabric. The shapes that could be achieved with cotton, gabardine, silk and gazar, and the clean, austere lines of this dress were made possible only by this cocktail of education and influence. When Courrèges left the house of Balenciaga, he took with him his colleague Coqueline Barrière, with whom he established the house of Courrèges and, later, married. Their first collection debuted in 1961, at a time when President Kennedy had decided to make the United States a supreme power, not just globally but universally, and when all eyes, hearts and minds had turned to the new frontier, space.

Fashion in the early 1960s had progressed little from the previous decade. Even the grand house of Dior had dismissed its young Creative Director, Yves Saint Laurent, in 1960, as his creations were considered too radical and uncommercial for their couture clients, choosing instead the classic designs of Marc Bohan. Courrèges bounded onto the scene at the start of the decade and caused a furore with his modernist, sculptural clothing and his unapologetic and vociferous approach to fashion, commenting 'Today's women are archaic in their appearance. I want to help them coincide with their time'.

Initially only able to offer his designs in haute couture, Courrèges felt trapped. Consequently, he was one of the first designers to focus on the development of prêt-à-porter so that women from all walks of life could wear Courrèges as an expression of not only who they were but also who they were going to be. Truly modern for his time, in an era when every designer dreamed of being allowed to call themself an haute couturier, Courrèges instead dreamed of being able to supply his designs to all women everywhere:

I realise how utterly immoral my high prices are and my public is far too limited. Soon I should have the possibility and the means to dress the women who do not have the means to dress in original Courrèges. Working women have always interested me the most. They belong to the present, the future.

OPPOSITE: ANDRÉ COURRÈGES AND MODELS WEARING PIECES FROM HIS SPRING 1968 HAUTE-COUTURE COLLECTION, PHOTOGRAPHED BY MANUEL LITRAN FOR PARIS MATCH, 1968

RIGHT: A WILLIAMVINTAGE COURRÈGES HAUTE-COUTURE DRESS IN IVORY SILK ORGANZA AND TANGERINE SILK FROM THE HAUTE-COUTURE COLLECTION, SPRING 1968

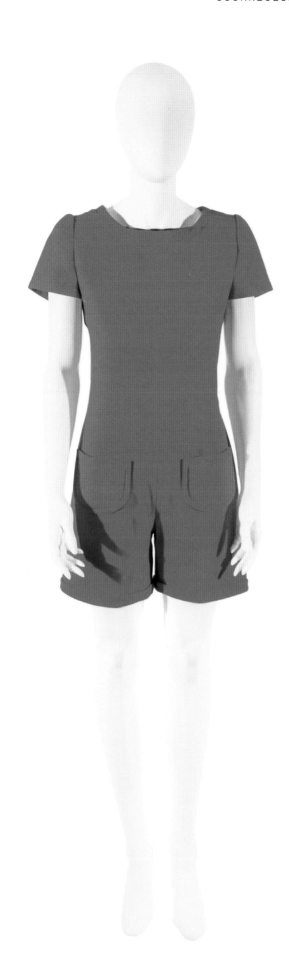

'Courrèges's look became synonymous with the dreams of the Western world, with Vogue's judgement of the 1964 "Moon Girl" collection being "Courrèges is tomorrow, begun today".'

In the same year that Courrèges launched his couture house and his strident new designs, President Kennedy addressed Congress and spoke of his desire to place a man on the moon. When the President made his 'We choose to go to the Moon' speech in 1962, the Space Race changed up a gear, with the world eager for new discoveries as America and Russia competed with each other to develop the necessary technologies. Then, startlingly, in September 1963 the young President made a speech in front of the General Assembly, suggesting that America and Russia should join forces to ensure that mankind made the leap as a whole. The world waited as it seemed that not only would another planet be visited, but also that the Cold War would come to an end, with Russia and the United States once again becoming allies. Eight weeks later, Lee Harvey Oswald ensured that the promising discussion between Presidents Kennedy and Khrushchev came to a sudden halt. Camelot lay in ruins as the world mourned the assassination of John F Kennedy at the age of 46, and the dream of an allied project was lost.

With the murder of the American President, the desire to reach the moon increased as it came to be regarded as an important part of the Kennedy legacy. After four intense years of dreams and competition to 'claim' space, seemingly all the arts united in the obsession. The New York World Fair of 1964 was dedicated to 'Man's achievement on a Shrinking Globe in an Expanding Universe', and the site of the fair shows an extraordinarily futuristic landscape of convex and concave structures in polished concrete and stucco, chrome and glass.

It was with this as the backdrop that Courrèges launched his 'Moon Girl' collection of 1964. Vinyl trims, ankle boots, futuristic eyewear and millinery, A-line dresses and shorter hems took the fashion world by storm. The Courrèges look

THIS PAGE: A WILLIAMVINTAGE COURRÈGES HAUTE-COUTURE PLAYSUIT IN RED WOOL WITH WELTED SEAMS AND REAR BELT, c1968

OPPOSITE: A COURRÈGES FASHION SHOOT, PHOTOGRAPHED BY BILL RAY FOR LIFE MAGAZINE, 1968

became synonymous with the dreams of the Western world, with *Vogue*'s judgement of the collection being, 'Courrèges is tomorrow, begun today'. The *beau monde* of the 1960s embraced the look. While previously there had been a separation between those who wore haute couture and those who wore prêt-à-porter, even among those in the public eye, Courrèges designs were photographed on Twiggy, the Duchess of Windsor, Diana Ross, Audrey Hepburn and Jackie Kennedy's sister, Princess Lee Radziwill.

The latter half of the 1960s saw no abate in the obsession with space. Public architecture became increasingly futuristic and television and film became focused upon other galaxies, with countless television series and movies being made involving aliens and intergalactic travel, including *Star Trek* in 1966 and both Roger Vadim's *Barbarella* and Stanley Kubrick's *2001: A Space Odyssey* in 1968. As all the arts remained focused on space, the house of Courrèges blossomed and grew in strength. As the decade drew to a close, the dream was finally realised when, on 20th July 1969, Neil Armstrong and Buzz Aldrin became the first humans to walk on another planet.

The Courrèges dress, with its clean lines, bold colour and almost uniform-like appearance, was a part of Courrèges's philosophy that the future had started and that women needed to dress for the world they were about to inhabit. His boldness spoke to other designers and soon Pierre Cardin, Emmanuelle Ungaro and Paco Rabanne were creating hypnotic, futuristic haute couture in Paris, while in London Mary Quant and John Bates led the charge in ready-to-wear. To this day, it is still hotly debated as to which of these designers could be said to have 'created' the mini dress, first seen in 1964. While today, when so many of the 1960s ideas of what the twenty-first century would hold seem so ridiculous, it is extraordinary that the Courrèges dress was precisely what Courrèges thought it would be: the way in which a twenty-first-century woman would choose to clothe herself.

OPPOSITE: DONYALE LUNA WEARING COURRÈGES HAUTE COUTURE, PHOTOGRAPHED BY HELMUT NEWTON FOR ELLE FRANCE, 1967

The Courrèges Legacy

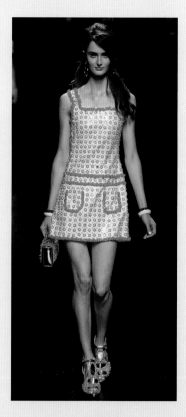

Miu Miu   *Moschino*   *Moschino*

Madame Grès

The Cult of the Goddess

A designer who held true to her beliefs and ideals, MADAME GRÈS ignored the constant winds of change in fashion and developed a style entirely her own.

While other dresses featured in this book are inherently modern, they are also representative of a particular generation of women and designers; not so this spectacular 1967 haute-couture dress by Madame Grès. Grès believed that 'Once one has found something of a personal and unique character, its execution must be exploited and pursued without stopping.' This sensual silk-jersey dress attests to her sensibility, not just in the late 1960s but throughout her sixty-year career.

The life of Madame Grès is shrouded in mystery. Her private affairs, business practices and partners, and, ultimately, the circumstances of her death remain hotly debated. It has been established that she was born in Paris in 1903 to haute-bourgeois parents and christened Germaine Émilie Krebs. The young Grès was educated in dance, sculpture, painting and music and while she hoped to become a sculptor, her family's disdain for the artistic life led her to embark upon a career within haute couture. Reportedly spending the 1920s working first as a seamstress and then as a designer within smaller houses in Paris, Grès opened a house in 1933 under the name Alix Barton, reflecting her first choice of moniker, Madame Alix. Following disagreements with her business partner, the house soon closed and the new house of Alix emerged.

By the late 1930s the folded, pleated, body-skimming works of Madame Alix had become sought-after creations, with positive reviews in both *Vogue* and *L'Officiel*. By 1934 the work of Alix had graced the cover of *Vogue*, house clients included Marlene Dietrich and Greta Garbo, and in 1935 *Vogue* described her sleeves 'pleated like a cathedral organ' and her dresses 'of thin white jersey net, [Alix] draping it into liquid folds'. Grès was a superb tailor, producing extraordinarily well-conceived and beautifully executed daywear, but it is the evening dresses in her preferred silk jersey that became her legacy.

TOP LEFT: A STATUE OF DEMETER, ATHENS, c500BC

LEFT: A PORTRAIT OF MADAME GRÈS WITH A MODEL, PHOTOGRAPHED BY EUGÈNE RUBIN, 1946

OPPOSITE: A WILLIAMVINTAGE MADAME GRÈS HAUTE-COUTURE DRESS IN BLACK SILK JERSEY, c1967

Well educated within the arts and with a latent desire to sculpt, Grès's imagination, like that of Mariano Fortuny before her, had been captured by the lure of Classical Greece. Whereas Fortuny was inspired specifically by the columnar dress of the *Charioteer of Delphi*, Grès's passion was more akin to that of the dancer Isadora Duncan, who saw within the ancient sculptures a mellifluous grace and undulating drapery, which could both conceal and reveal the body in equal measure – a dichotomy that was to become the Grès signature. While this dress also owes a great deal to the *Charioteer*, it is impossible not to compare it to the caryatids of the Erechtheion on the Acropolis of Athens, dating from *c*420BC. That they must also have been a source of inspiration for Grès can be seen in the generous use of fabric and the fullness of folds at the waistline at the rear of this dress, with its extraordinary cowled back and loosely gathered silk. While her contemporaries and competitors would change their silhouette and sartorial language with each passing season, Grès would instead focus her energies upon the dresses she adored, holding to her belief that 'for a dress to survive from one era to the next, it must be marked with an extreme purity'.

With an obsessive nature and a desire to create perfect form, Grès approached haute couture in a manner similar to that of a sculptor, working the fabric directly onto a body and manipulating each minuscule fold until she was satisfied. Over the decades she gained tremendous understanding of the way fabric would respond to the female form from her initial designs. Composed of one continuous piece of fabric, the form and shape of the dress would emerge as she draped, gathered, pleated and stitched the fine material into position, just as one would carve a sculpture from a block of stone. Likewise, the hem would be cut with a pair of scissors and left unfinished in an honest evocation of the Hellenic clothing she adored. This dress, constructed in the finest sheer black silk jersey, is the result of almost forty years of experimenting and perfecting that approach. With Ancient Greece so clearly its inspiration, it shows why Grès is forever associated with a gown commonly known as 'the Goddess dress'.

With Grès's almost preternatural ability to convert six feet of fabric into six inches of finished pleating, each seemingly ethereal dress could contain up to twenty-five yards of silk jersey. This lavish use of fabric was a cause for concern during the Second World War. The Chambre Syndicale de la Haute Couture had successfully argued with the Nazis that haute couture should remain active during the occupation of Paris, but they had agreed to police the quantity of fabric used by designers. Grès, however, objected to such interference. In 1941, having fled Paris after the Nazi occupation of the city, Grès was summoned back to prove

that she was not of Jewish descent. Such was her anger that she decided to abandon couture, sell her shares in the house of Alix and join her husband, the artist Serge Czerefkow, in his new home. This decision was all the more startling given that Czerefkow had already emigrated to Tahiti and taken a mistress. Persuaded to stay in France by her fellow designers, Grès established a new atelier; however, appalled by the investigation into her racial history and passionate about her craft, she refused Nazi clients and ignored any demands put upon her regarding fabric rationing. For her 1944 show Grès took the inspiration of classical drapery to its apex when she 'hid' her finest and most extravagant dresses within the niches of her atelier, posing them as statues, and offered a palette of red, white and blue, the colours of the French Tricolour and an overt statement of national independence.

While Grès had long been inspired by the fluid sculptures of Greece, the timing of the opening of her new atelier could not have been better. The Greek couturier Jean Dessès was already active in Paris and his work would evoke an alternate language based upon Classical Greece and ancient Egypt, while in 1943 the Metropolitan Museum of Art in New York held a major exhibition entitled 'The Greek Revival in the United States', which included contemporary fashion based upon the antique. Grès's new atelier, its name an anagram of that of her husband Serge, had opened in the darkest time Paris had seen since the French Revolution and would be the only couture house created in the years of the German occupation. The house of Grès had been born, and with it the name Madame Grès.

Soon after the launch of her house and the revived global interest in Greek culture and fashion, Dior showed his first collection in 1947 to great acclaim. His vision was detested by Grès. The nipped-in waist, exaggerated hips, vast skirts and 'flower women' of this new King of Couture were anathema to her. While Dior placed women firmly back in the corsets that Grès felt belonged in the past, her work shifted fractionally. Still maintaining the 'purity' she adored, her haute couture became more fitted during the 1950s, with a greater emphasis on the waist and an increased use of boning. Her fundamental vision, however, did not falter and her draped masterpieces continued to find an audience. That such a singular approach to clothing survived for so many decades is testament to Grès's extraordinary technical skill and the creation of dresses that held innate appeal to women, irrespective of the current dictats of the season. The Goddess dress was timeless, elegant and Hellenic, and had become a look so associated with Grès that she maintained a devoted clientele. Grès had

OPPOSITE: A MADAME GRÈS HAUTE-COUTURE DRESS MODELLED BY LISA FONSSAGRIEVES, PHOTOGRAPHED BY EUGÈNE RUBIN FOR HARPER'S BAZAAR, *c1940*

'Gathered, draped, pleated and flowing, the goddess dress was timeless, elegant and Hellenic.'

become a bastion of haute couture with a house as revered as those of Chanel and Dior. Her unfaltering and obdurate vision garnered respect from her fellow designers and the Légion d'Honneur award from the French government. In 1959 Grès launched a perfume that was so successful it transformed the power and wealth of her atelier. Fittingly for a designer who walked to the beat of her own drum, the scent was called Cabochard, the French for 'obstinate'.

The house of Grès had survived the revolution of the New Look, but the 1960s held even greater challenges, with rapidly changing silhouettes, the emergence of pop culture and, most importantly, the arrival of prêt-à-porter. Madame Grès viewed her dresses and the process behind their creation as a form of art. Despite producing a succession of short-lived prêt-à-porter collections, she considered it impossible to create dresses for unknown, faceless women, and went as far as to call the process 'a prostitution'. With a client list that included Jacqueline Kennedy and Barbra Streisand, the house of Grès remained a stalwart of haute couture; in 1967 *Vogue* wrote that 'Her customers tend to consider a Grès dress as a work of art, not just something to wear to a dinner party'. This dress of the same year is no exception. With its gathered, draped and cowled silk jersey caressing the body and its transparency allowing for a tantalising glimpse of the naked form within it, the dress is a lesson in stealthy eroticism. While Grès had long incorporated areas of exposed skin within her designs so that they seemed to be a natural extension of the dress – referred to by Harold Koda as 'windows on to the body' – in this example she took the idea to a new level. Despite its classical origins and its seemingly demure appearance, the dress is designed to expose the lower curve of the spine when viewed from the side, the shoulder blades when viewed from the rear, and the meeting point of the breasts when viewed from the front, making it both intoxicatingly sexual and coolly elegant.

Despite the success of Cabochard and subsequent fragrances, increased distribution and being made President of the Chambre Syndicale de la Haute Couture in 1970, during the 1960s Grès had embarked upon a series of decisions that would lead to the collapse of both her house and fortune. While she

THIS PAGE: A MADAME GRÈS HAUTE-COUTURE DRESS, PHOTOGRAPHED BY GUY BOURDIN FOR VOGUE ITALIA, *MAY 1975*

OVERLEAF: A MADAME GRÈS HAUTE-COUTURE DRESS, PHOTOGRAPHED BY GEORGE PLATT LYNES, c1940

adapted her output to cater to the millionaire hippies of the 1960s, her repulsion for prêt-à-porter ensured that at a time when the work of her fellow designers was coveted by a younger, international generation, she remained fatally Paris-centric and sadly did not take note when, in 1964, Brigitte Bardot stated that 'Couture is for the grannies'. A series of appointments within the house of Grès led to financial disagreements, broken contracts, multi-million dollar financial settlements and the effective strip-mining of the house.

Grès, at heart a designer with a singular passion for the haute couture she adored, sold first her perfume business and then the majority stake of the house itself, her two greatest and most secure assets. In the pursuit of purity and perfect form, Grès showed both her strength and weakness; she was an artist not a business woman, and by the 1980s her house was beset by chaos. In 1986 Grès was expelled by the Chambre Syndicale de la Haute Couture for non-payment of fees, despite being its President, and in 1988, having failed to pay rent for two years, the Grès atelier was forcibly closed down. In the course of a day, the rooms of the Grès atelier were stripped and the current haute-couture collection was tossed into refuse bags and thrown onto the streets. The 'sphinx of fashion' had stayed silent too long; her reclusive manner, obstinate ways and inability to change with the times leading to the collapse of one of the most iconic couture houses in the world, a

commercial entity that, if it had been managed differently, could have evolved into a luxury house to equal its contemporaries, Dior, Chanel and Balenciaga.

The greatest irony in the saga of the house of Grès is that at its heart lay a woman whose life was inspired by Ancient Greece and whose death is worthy of Euripides. Choosing to live in the shadows not the limelight, Grès refused to attend retrospectives of her work and she bought up every copy of books published about her house, determined to protect her privacy and aura of mystery. In 1994 the Costume Institute at the Metropolitan Museum of Art announced a Grès retrospective and was delighted when she wrote to express her thanks for 'not forgetting about her'. A flurry of press releases announced her approval, and there was a even whisper that the aged lady herself might attend. However, the renewed press interest led to a shocking denouement: the letter so valued by the curators was a forgery written by Grès's daughter. The woman who had inspired Rei Kawakubo, Issey Miyake, Rick Owens and so many other designers of the late twentieth century had died, alone and penniless, in a nursing home in France more than a year before, her grave unmarked and her daughter, inexplicably, maintaining the pretence that her mother was alive. The 'sphinx of fashion' had died as she had lived, yet her extraordinary designs, like that other mythical creature the phoenix, are continually reborn and reinterpreted.

The Grès Legacy

Giambattista Valli   *Valentino*   *Akris*

Halston

The Chaos
of Change

Few pieces of clothing are as symbolic of the 1970s as this sequinned pyjama suit and few designers are as representative of the decade itself as ROY HALSTON, its creator.

While his daywear set the tone for modern American chic, Halston was the label of choice for when the sun went down and this suit epitomises his opulent, unerring eye. Created from blue silk georgette set with thousands of midnight-blue sequins, the suit is simplicity itself. Comprising a pair of straight-legged trousers paired with an oversized masculine shirt and finished with a thin, sequinned belt to enhance the wearer's waist, it encapsulates the language of 1970s nights like no other and is a lesson in fluid, languid glamour.

The fashions of the 1970s have long been polarised into cliché; from the polyester-fuelled disco scene of *Saturday Night Fever* and the Bacchic excesses of a gilded youth in the legendary New York club Studio 54 to the 'fashion crimes' of mass-produced, man-made fabrics and cheap labour. However, the decade was far more complex and the work of Halston beautifully represents the era and its frenetic change.

Devastatingly handsome and standing six feet four inches tall, the Indiana-raised Roy Halston Frowick started his career in fashion first as a window dresser and then as a milliner; his transition to womenswear was achieved after great earlier successes. While many associate Halston solely with the 1970s, he first appeared in American *Vogue* in 1961 after designing the famous pillbox hat worn by Jackie Kennedy for her husband's inauguration as President of the United States, and his star was on the rise long before his clothing achieved global acclaim.

Throughout the 1960s Halston nurtured a client list of *grandes dames* who lapped up his creations, and amongst his burgeoning coterie of the great and the powerful, he also sought out the friendship of Charles James. America's master couturier on a par with the greatest names of European couture such as Balenciaga and Dior, James was a formidable force. The two men found a common theme in the love of superb technical construction, which was far more important to them than embellishment or artifice. James was famed for his pared-back, supremely well-executed day wear that focused upon exemplary tailoring, while Halston said in 1980 that he saw his role in fashion as, 'getting rid of all the extra details that didn't work – bows that didn't tie, buttons that didn't button, zippers that didn't zip, wrap dresses that didn't

ABOVE: PAPARAZZI SHOTS OF STUDIO 54, WITH GUESTS INCLUDING ANDY WARHOL, JERRY HALL, ELTON JOHN, LIZA MINNELLI AND ROY HALSTON

OPPOSITE: A WILLIAMVINTAGE HALSTON TROUSER SUIT IN SILK ORGANZA AND MIDNIGHT-BLUE SEQUINS, c1975

[154]

wrap – I've always hated things that don't work'. The two men were kindred spirits and after Halston launched his first womenswear collection and store in 1968, he hired the older, fabled couturier as a consultant designer. Their initial collaborations were not positively received and their relationship, both personal and professional, never recovered. James left an indelible mark upon Halston. After the accessorised pop-culture look of the 1960s, which was obsessed with the fresh and epicene boy-girl, Halston was in position to shape the way women of the next generation dressed. This trouser suit, for all its sequins and glamour, perfectly represents Halston's desire to 'get rid of all the details' and allow the simplicity of beautifully tailored, flowing silk to speak for itself. It is a lesson in artful, confident execution, without the bows, trims, flounces and loud prints used by so many of Halston's contemporaries, which he felt hid the woman within the clothes rather than showcased her.

The early 1970s saw a relinquishing of the aesthetics of the past. The futurism of the mid-1960s and its French ambassadors, André Courrèges, Pierre Cardin and Emanuel Ungaro, had led into a post-Woodstock, post-Vietnam romanticism, espoused by its British ambassadors, Thea Porter, Bill Gibb and Ossie Clark. Halston did not need to imagine the next stage in evolution, nor did he try to change the way women dressed, but rather he created clothing for the women he already knew. Armed with a client list of moneyed, urbane women and blessed with good looks and a gregarious personality, Halston and his designs reflected the change in fashion itself. Halston stripped away the matched, homogeneous look of the mid-1960s and used the inspiration point of the later 1960s, a romanticised take on 1930s tailoring, to create a new and sophisticated language that had not been seen since the heady days of the Art Deco period, with its body-skimming bias cuts, fluid forms and louche glamour.

A turning point in the perception of glamour during the decade was the birth of the paparazzi. Previously movie stars and politicians had been carefully controlled and their pictures were often no more than staged studio shots, but the 1970s saw a far greater accessibility and images of the most famous people in the world travelling, partying and living their life away from the gilded screen were available to everyone. Halston soon realised that it was not just his finished collections that would determine how successful his brand was, but also his life and how he lived it.

Where previously designers had taken a calculated decision to extend their market share by launching into perfumery, eyewear and ancillary products but keeping their own image and private life away from the buying public, Halston's persona was at the epicentre of his brand and it was

TOP: ROY HALSTON WITH ELIZABETH TAYLOR, WEARING A HALSTON SEQUINNED TROUSER SUIT, 1974

ABOVE: ROY HALSTON WITH MARISA BERENSON, WEARING A HALSTON BEADED DRESS, 1978

OPPOSITE: MICK JAGGER AND BIANCA JAGGER, WEARING A HALSTON RED SEQUINNED DRESS AND CAP, 1974

A PORTRAIT OF ROY HALSTON AT HIS MANHATTAN HOME,
PHOTOGRAPHED BY HARRY BENSON FOR LIFE MAGAZINE, 1978

the paparazzi images of him and his iconic friends that fuelled public obsession. While he too launched sell-out perfumes, accessories and licensed ranges, his success was cemented by his customers' desire to have a 'Halston life', which by 1973 had become synonymous with urbane, sophisticated glamour. Halston made sure that he lived that dream.

By the mid-1970s Halston counted the most famous women in the world as both friends and clients, including celebrity supermodels Marisa Berenson, Rene Russo, Anjelica Huston, Beverly Johnson and Jerry Hall, film stars Elizabeth Taylor and Liza Minnelli, socialites Nan Kempner and Babe Paley, and former First Ladies Jackie Kennedy Onassis and Betty Ford. This was the time when the class system was being torn down, when pedigrees mattered less and when the previously separate spheres of film, fashion, art and politics merged. Halston was present for it all, either in the form of a swathe of silk or the man himself, staring at the camera lens.

As barriers were coming down and worlds were colliding, huge social changes were afoot. The National Association for the Advancement of Colored People had entrenched itself globally in its campaign for equal rights and opportunities. After legislative successes, the 1960s and 1970s saw the rise of the black model, with Halston favourite African-American Beverly Johnson being the first black model to appear on the cover of American *Vogue* in 1974 and French *Elle* in 1975, and African-American Pat Cleveland ruling the runway for the house of Saint Laurent in Paris. Black film and literature bloomed with the writing of Alice Walker, Toni Morrison, Maya Angelou and Alex Halley, and for the first time black actors, directors and producers could undertake film work based upon their talent and expertise and not simply upon the need for caricature.

Just as the Black Power Movement and the Black Arts Movement flourished throughout the 1970s, so too did the Gay Rights Movement. Following the Stonewall riots in New York in 1969, the 1970s saw the movement grow, and a breaking down of cultural and legal barriers began worldwide. In 1973 the American Psychiatric Association removed homosexuality from its *Diagnostic and Statistical Manual of Mental Disorders*; in 1974 and 1975 Australia and the majority of American states decriminalised homosexuality and, with the elections of Kathy Kozachenko in 1974 and Harvey Milk in 1977 to state board level, the first openly gay politicians were enabled.

There can be no greater record of the 1970s than the paparazzi shots taken within Studio 54. Hedonistic as the parties may have been, they were a celebration of a world that had opened up, and hidden within the excess of the elite was a greater acceptance and a greater freedom for all. The most iconic images show Liza Minnelli and Elizabeth Taylor seated beside former First Lady Betty Ford, with all three women wearing a sequinned Halston couture dress. Halston understood the camera lens and knew his stripped-back glamour and use of sequins and bugle beads would make every paparazzi shot something beautiful, dazzling and iconic. When Bianca Jagger entered her thirtieth birthday celebrations wearing a Halston dress, atop a white stallion being led into Studio 54 by four naked, oiled men, it was to a crowd including Halston, partying with Andy Warhol, Grace Jones and Jerry Hall. Halston was present in every way throughout the 1970s, dressing the key players, appearing on stage personally and writing a great part of the story himself. However, there was a stranger in the room.

While 'patient zero' was not diagnosed until October 1980, the HIV virus had been gestating throughout the 1970s, the decade that had witnessed a breaking down of barriers, increased drug use, a higher level of promiscuity and the advent of the contraceptive pill. This meant that at a pivotal time the disease had spread unchecked and many of the faces of Studio 54 and the creative industries in the 1970s and early 1980s were its victim, including the handsome, talented Roy Halston Frowick. It is difficult to look at the 1970s and the role Halston played without being conscious that this is what the world looked like immediately before the most aggressive, virulent disease known to man took hold. Yet his creative genius, timeless design ideals and innate understanding of luxury fashion and the development of a fashion lifestyle still inspire the greatest designers of the twenty-first century. Speaking about a visit to Halston's impeccable home, design icon Tom Ford said:

I was fortunate to have been in the townhouse in the early 1980s when I first arrived in New York and I remember being stunned by it. Clean, simple, streamlined ... It really had an effect on me. In many ways I have integrated this design philosophy into my life.

The Halston Legacy

Gucci

Lanvin

Jean Paul Gaultier

Saint Laurent

The Body Beautiful

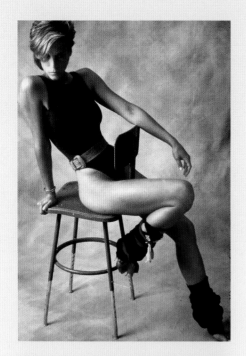

An YVES SAINT LAURENT dress can never be said to represent all that is Saint Laurent; no one piece can be held up as his eternal signature in the manner of a Dior or Courrèges.

Yves Saint Laurent and his aesthetics spanned the decades, often pre-empting changes in society and the impact they had upon a woman and her wardrobe. Within each decade his work was entirely different, becoming the hallmark of its age.

From the Saint Laurent Autumn/Winter 1981 collection, this dress is a vision of sparkling micro-sequins contrasted with the soft sheen of silk satin and finished with a vast, transparent skirt of light-absorbing black tulle. Where Halston would create a sequinned dress to act like a sartorial firework, and while this dress and many of Halston's were influenced by 1930s Art Deco, there is a greater sense of dark glamour and stealth here. For all the luxurious fabrics, there is simplicity and austerity to the design. Slinky, sequinned dresses were nothing new in 1981, but this dress demonstrates one dramatic change: the type of body a woman was expected to have in order to wear it.

Adorned with sequins to catch the light as they moved, the columnar flapper dresses of the 1920s had been worn by women who understood that their physique needed to be '*à la garçonne*' and for whom the word diet did not exist – the phrase used at the time being the far more literal 'starving down'. According to fashion lore, women bound down their busts to fit the unforgiving, shapeless silhouette and even removed wisdom teeth in order to increase the line of their cheekbones in an attempt to look as emaciated as possible.

Following the Great Depression and the Second World War, the notion of the perfect female silhouette changed radically. From Pierre Balmain's petrol-like sheaths of the 1950s to Norman Norrell's showstoppers of the 1960s and Marilyn Monroe's unforgettable Jean Louis dress worn to serenade President Kennedy on his birthday in 1962, sequinned dresses all had a common theme; they were designed to draw attention to the curves of a woman, taking the eye directly from bust to hip and thigh in a symphony of rounded, full flesh. In the case of Monroe's dress, it fitted her so tightly she had to be stitched into it in order to showcase her pneumatic body. For dresses of this era, the sequin was the final embellishment upon a creation featuring girdles, corsets, internal waistbands, cup supports and every device possible to lift, support and encase the fuller figure to devastating, Rubenesque affect.

TOP: JAMIE LEE CURTIS IN A PRESS SHOT FOR THE ULTIMATE AEROBICS MOVIE PERFECT, 1985

ABOVE: JANE FONDA, PHOTOGRAPHED BY HARRY LANGDON, 1985

OPPOSITE: A WILLIAMVINTAGE YVES SAINT LAURENT ENSEMBLE IN SILK SATIN, TULLE AND SEQUINS, 1981

OVERLEAF: AN YVES SAINT LAURENT HAUTE-COUTURE DRESS, PHOTOGRAPHED BY BILL RAY FOR LIFE MAGAZINE, 1968

During the shifting decade of the 1960s, it was not long before the ideal silhouette changed once more. The adolescent 'girl-woman' took hold, with Twiggy as the benchmark for androgynous cool in the years leading up to the 1970s. A time of heady excess and abandon alongside 'Age of Aquarius' ideology, the 1970s was perhaps the first decade in which women had the freedom to choose their weight or let nature dictate their body shape. The more forgiving lines of Halston and the latent 1930s revival allowed for a greater freedom that hid the underweight and the overweight and flatter those women who let their own bodies decide the form they took.

This sequinned Saint Laurent was not designed for the starved-down look of the 1920s, the buxom bombshell of the 1950s or the more natural body of the 1970s, but for the latest desirable silhouette, that of the honed, lean athlete. The bodice bears no internal supports, no bust shaping and no arm cover. The wearer of the dress would see within it a way of showcasing not only a fabulous gown, but also her fabulous body, honed by the latest wisdom in diet and exercise.

By the end of the 1970s, with Freud's much-debated 'id' in a permanent state of hangover from so many years of partying, drink and drugs, there was a shift towards health and physical exercise. From its early days as a niche hobby, the attainment of the 'gym body' soon became an obsession for fashion-loving couture buyers. By 1980 health clubs and gyms were appearing in towns and cities around the world and the change was being noted by film, television and music. The biggest film of the year, with six Academy Award nominations, was the dance-led drama *Fame*. The year Saint Laurent designed this dress, *Jane Fonda's Workout Book* was published and Olivia Newton-John released *Physical*. With a music video featuring the singer working out surrounded by near-naked, muscled men, the title track went platinum. This video was one of the first aired by a new television channel, MTV; the impact of the video and its marriage of chart songs with choreography further promoted the idea of exercising to music. Aerobics and the pursuit of the fat-free gym body became a worldwide phenomenon.

Saint Laurent's friend and muse Catherine Deneuve said of him, 'Yves designed clothes for women who lead double lives'. While making reference to her 1967 film *Belle de Jour*, for which he designed her wardrobe, she also conveys a message about the house of Saint Laurent. While other designers polarised the roles of women – Mugler and his vamp, Courrèges and his Moon Girl, Dior and his flower-women – Saint Laurent understood the duality of the female psyche; he realised that a woman could be mother, daughter, worker, lover, fighter and dancer, and fulfil all these roles within the course of a day rather than a lifetime. In designing this dress with a simple, unsupported camisole top and a skirt so transparent that hard-earned lean legs would not be hidden, Saint Laurent understood the new shape of glamour and what would be expected of the evening gown at the dawn of the 1980s, and he delivered it perfectly. Feel the burn.

The Saint Laurent Legacy

Alexandre Vauthier

Oscar de la Renta

Dior

Ferré

Dior and the
Rise of the East

This dress, by GIANFRANCO FERRÉ for Dior, is emblematic of a recurring theme first seen at the house when under the direction of Dior himself: the allure and mysticism of the East.

In 1955 Christian Dior said 'Couture ... has become the expression of a personality, that of the head of the fashion house.' His assertion was prophetic; the house of Dior is as famous for its designers as it is for its designs. While the eras of Dior, Yves Saint Laurent, Marc Bohan, John Galliano and Raf Simons are all reviewed, revered and reviled, season by season and piece by piece, there is another designer who is often overlooked, despite having completed fifteen collections for the house – Gianfranco Ferré.

This striking evening gown, designed by Ferré for his very last collection at Dior in Autumn/Winter 1996, is representative of not only his design ideals but also the appeal and glamour of the East, a theme that had persisted at the house since the time of Dior. Constructed in silk and velvet the colour of a Burmese ruby, the dress was part of an haute-couture collection entitled 'Passion indienne', featuring rich jewel tones, gold embellishment and paisley, combined with cardamom, turmeric, mango and the bright, saturated colour known universally as 'Indian pink'. While the dress is an example of Dior haute couture at its most formal and in the tradition of its *robes de grand gala*, its spiralling, folded silk and asymmetric finish simulates the wrapping of a body and is the ultimate Western evocation of the Indian sari.

Gianfranco Ferré and his time at Dior is often considered unimportant by comparison with the other great designers who have been at the helm of the house. However, this has more to do with the way in which fashion had finally become a part of the corporate animal. In 1985, only two years before Ferré was appointed head of Dior, the companies of Louis Vuitton and Moët Hennessy merged to create the consortium known as LVMH, a multinational luxury goods conglomerate that aimed to harness and acquire the greatest houses in the world. The primary major shareholders of the fashion houses Dior, Givenchy, Fendi, Céline, Pucci, Berluti, Loewe and Kenzo, the champagne houses Veuve Clicquot, Krug, Dom Pérignon, Ruinart and Moët & Chandon, and the jewellers De Beers, Chaumet, Fred and Bulgari, LVMH is not so much a part of the luxury landscape as its landlord. Immensely powerful and with extraordinary business acumen from its inception, LVMH

ABOVE: GOUACHE DRAWINGS BY VASANTI RAJIM, RAHIM DECCANI AND AN UNKNOWN ARTIST, c1690–1790

OPPOSITE: A WILLIAMVINTAGE DIOR HAUTE-COUTURE DRESS BY GIANFRANCO FERRÉ IN RED SILK VELVET AND RED SILK SATIN, AUTUMN/WINTER 1996

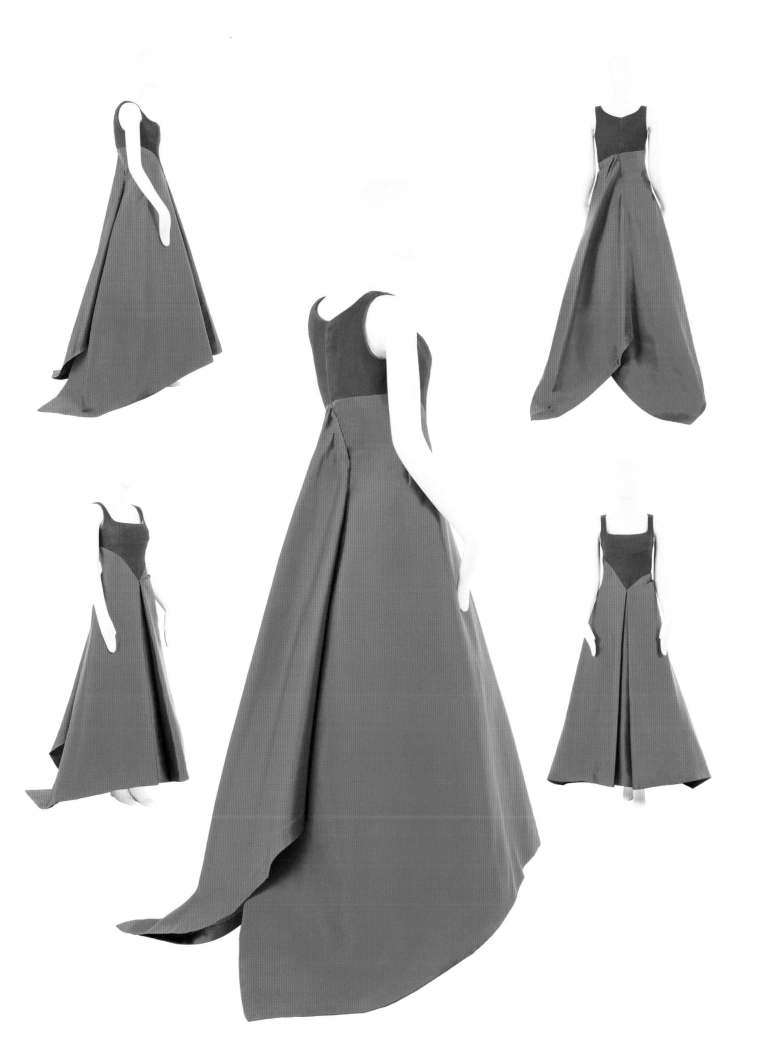

was able to bring strategic, streamlined business practices into industries that had often foundered due to being based solely on creative genius. However, while this uber-brand was lauded for bringing much-needed corporate expertise into the world of fashion, there are those who felt that the houses under its control lost the spirit and language that made them unique. Legend has it that when he was appointed head of the house of Dior, Gianfranco Ferré was told by Bernard Arnault, chairman of the newly formed LVMH, to 'Do some Dior'.

At the end of the 1980s and throughout the 1990s, just as the structure of fashion houses was changing, so too were its offerings. The world of haute couture struggled to find relevance as the popularity, availability and sophistication of prêt-à-porter increased. While the 1990s may have been an era of corporate domination, it was also a time when designers were looking to the East and Far East for inspiration. From the clean lines of Donna Karan and Calvin Klein to the buildings of the Chinese-born architect I M Pei, the growth of minimalism and adoption by the West of the ancient principles of Feng Shui, it seemed that as daily life became increasingly capitalist and 'Westernised', the world looked to the East for its heart and soul.

In choosing Ferré as the new head of Dior, LVMH had appointed an Italian to the most iconic couture house in France, and selected a man who could deliver his Italian understanding of glamour with a technical approach to fashion derived from his training as an architect. Ultimately, in his final collection, he also displayed the understanding and respect of a man who had lived in India for nearly six years.

Born in Milan in 1945 and initially trained in architecture, Gianfranco Ferré had an eye that considered each and every detail in a way that rendered him not only a superb technical architect but also led him quickly to the applied arts. His first foray into fashion was the creation of jewellery for his female friends. Bold, sculptural and earnest, the pieces were spotted by boutique owners before Anna Piaggi, the legendary stylist and writer, discovered them and became one of Ferré's earliest advocates. Ferré developed a role as an expert in the design and production of accessories and clothing, and travelled extensively, not only for Italian fashion houses but also for the Italian government's trade department, spending time in India sourcing production locations, pools of talented workers and superb textiles. Ferré often commented that it was this period of his life that gave him his greatest inspiration as a fashion designer, not just for the finished garment but for the way in which colour, texture and embellishment formed a part of the entire design process.

Gianfranco Ferré founded his house in 1978 and received his first accolade in *Vogue* in 1979 before launching menswear collections in 1983. The first time he was offered the position

of head at Dior in 1985, Ferré turned it down, only to be asked again, successfully, in 1988. Ferré's time at Dior caused great polarity amongst fashion's cognoscenti; viewed as either an era of grand craftsmanship for the old guard of couture clients or conservative, anodyne design for a disappearing demographic, continuing to inspire debate.

For this last collection by Ferré for Dior, shown to a soundtrack of sitar and sarinda music, Ferré returned to his years spent in India and produced a dress that seamlessly fuses the heritage and language of Monsieur Dior with his own love of the East and, in so doing, continued a story laid out by Dior himself at the inception of the house. A tremendous success from its first collection in 1947,

ABOVE: THE DUCHESS OF WINDSOR WEARING DIOR HAUTE COUTURE FROM THE AUTUMN/WINTER 1950 COLLECTION, PHOTOGRAPHED BY CECIL BEATON, 1951

OPPOSITE: A DIOR HAUTE-COUTURE DRESS WITH HINDU-INSPIRED EMBROIDERY BY REBÉ, PHOTOGRAPHED BY PHILIPPE POTTIER FOR L'OFFICIEL, 1955

OVERLEAF: YASMEEN GHAURI ON THE DIOR RUNWAY FOR 'PASSION INDIENNES', AUTUMN/WINTER 1996

the house of Dior drew celebrity clients almost immediately and one wonders if the Duchess of Windsor and Marlene Dietrich were aware that a number of the dresses they purchased were inspired by the Indian Empire. Dior's Winter 1947 dinner dress 'Chandernagor', purchased by Dietrich, was named after a city in French Indochina, while his Winter 1948 dress 'Lahore', made famous by the Duchess of Windsor, was named in honour of the city in the newly formed Pakistan. Several years later, Dior's extraordinary dress of 1954 'Palmyre' would be purchased by the Duchess of Windsor and its ornate crystal embellishment is entirely influenced by Indian design. For all the hyperbole surrounding Dior and his New Look, a great many of his sartorial triumphs were brought about not by the style and panache of the French but by his love of the East and, in particular, of Moghul decoration. In this final collection, Ferré not only revived Dior's interest in the East, but also, conversely, set the scene for his replacement. John Galliano would take the language of Dior and apply it to his own obsession for the romance and erotica of the East, taking the house to a new level of post-modern excess with an almost kaleidoscopic sense of adventure within his glorious haute couture. However, this dress also holds within it evidence of another point of inspiration clearly shared by Ferré and the incumbent Galliano, the work of the earlier couturier Charles James.

Little known in comparison to the mythic status that surrounds his French contemporaries, James was a master couturier but one lacking the commercial prowess of Dior. While achieving a cult-like status within the American elite at the time, his house produced less than nine-hundred pieces in over thirty years. Were it not for a handful of devoted clients, who understood the extraordinary devotion James applied to each finished dress, his house would have foundered. Through their patronage and through the artful collaboration of James, his clients and the Brooklyn Museum Costume Collection, more than a hundred of his finest works have been saved for posterity; such is his importance and influence that the 2014 Met Gala was held in honour of his work. James was obsessed with the engineering and architectural possibilities of a dress and the juxtaposition of countless fabrics within one garment, and his legacy is apparent in this haute-couture dress by Ferré for Dior, which is inspired as much by James's masterful ball gowns of 1949 as by any 'passion Indiennes' Ferré may have had. One can only wonder what Ferré thought of Galliano's subsequent collections, so close were they in inspiration to his own; Galliano payed homage to James throughout his work but with overt references in both his 2004 and 2010 collections. The time of Ferré had ended and another chapter had begun, but the passions and experiences of the Italian had already become part of the common language of the house of Dior.

The Ferré Legacy

Marchesa

Marchesa

Marchesa

McQueen

The Petites Mains of Paris

An haute-couture dress designed by ALEXANDER MCQUEEN provides the best explanation for the survival of the haute-couture industry into the twenty-first century.

TOP: PEGGY GUGGENHEIM WEARING PAUL POIRET HAUTE COUTURE, PHOTOGRAPHED BY MAN RAY, 1925

ABOVE: AUTUMN FLOWERS BY GEORGES DE FEURE, c1915

OPPOSITE: A WILLIAMVINTAGE ALEXANDER MCQUEEN FOR GIVENCHY HAUTE-COUTURE DRESS IN DOVE-GREY SILK CREPE AND CHAIN MAIL BY LESAGE, SPRING/SUMMER 1998

Long seen as the preserve of the wealthy elite, the validity of haute couture had been in question for more than forty years before the young British designer Alexander McQueen appeared and changed its role forever. By the 1960s prêt-à-porter had come into its own and by the 1980s haute couture was viewed as no more than conspicuous consumption in a decade of conflict and economic crises. With its very existence in peril, couture shows were becoming a parade of excess to empty gilded seats, as flocks of buyers defected to the increasingly sophisticated ready-to-wear collections. Haute couture lay exposed, a confused and archaic leftover from the golden age of the mid-twentieth century. Then came Alexander McQueen. While his life and work can never be contained within one chapter of a book, nor a single dress fully explain his talent and artistic genius, this gown is testament to the man referred to as the *enfant terrible* of British fashion taking the helm of one of the most hallowed and sophisticated couture houses in the world. It was a volatile and unhappy marriage, but one from which McQueen emerged a changed man, strident and more artistically powerful than he could ever have imagined.

A post-modernist in his irreverent use of historic detail, an anarchist in his use and abuse of form and shape, a revolutionary in challenging the expectations of the couture audience and a classicist in his understanding and execution of cut and tailoring, McQueen will always be a paradox. With early collections named 'Jack the Ripper Stalks his Victims' (1992) and 'Highland Rape' (Autumn/Winter 1995), along with his later 'The Widows of Culloden' (Autumn/Winter 2006) and 'In Memory of Elizabeth Howe, Salem 1692' (Autumn/Winter 2007), McQueen was forever exploring the emotional and visual ties from the present to the past, whether through colour, texture and cut or the way in which his shows were staged. An Alexander McQueen show became part of the performing arts as much as fashion, and his seminal Spring/Summer 2001 'VOSS' collection confirmed his role as both an artistic and sartorial master. In staging 'VOSS', McQueen had constructed a box stage, which initially acted as a mirror forcing the audience to look at themselves and question

their own appearance and the way in which they objectified both fashion and the models they were there to judge. However, when the lighting changed they were presented with a dark tableau. Within the box stage Michelle Olley, writer and founder of the Skin Two rubber fetish night, was revealed naked, wearing a gas mask and trapped with hundreds of moths in a near re-creation of Joel-Peter Witkin's nightmarish photograph *Sanitarium*. With 'VOSS', as with many of his shows, McQueen transported his audience into a febrile, vulnerable state where his vision could inspire adoration and repulsion in equal measure and where, above all, he was able to challenge the perception of beauty and what fashion was supposed to convey.

In the midst of developing his own house and with a growing reputation as the outspoken wunderkind of fashion, McQueen was suddenly appointed to a role that shocked the fashion world. In 1996 Bernard Arnault, Chairman of LVMH, decided to remove John Galliano from his position at Givenchy and instate him at Dior. Arnault also decided that Galliano's replacement at the aristocratic house of Givenchy should be Alexander McQueen. Initially unwilling to take the position, after a long and forceful negotiation with Arnault

and with a substantial salary agreed, McQueen entered into what would be a brief and complicated tenure at Givenchy, announced in October 1996.

McQueen delivered his first collection for the house of Givenchy in Spring 1997, only for it to be deemed a failure; to the fury of Arnault, he went on to tell the press that he too thought the collection was 'crap'. That his second collection in Autumn/Winter 1997 did not fare any better was of great importance. For Arnault, LVMH and the house of Givenchy, it was vital that public perception of the brand improved and that sales increased. For McQueen, having had so many years of extraordinary praise lavished upon him, the feeling of failure was a source of constant pain and unwanted pressure.

This exquisitely embellished silk-crepe dress, a part of that all-important, make-or-break haute-couture collection for Givenchy in Spring/Summer 1998, signalled a dynamic change in both McQueen's mastery of haute couture and the way in which he subverted his language for the house of Givenchy. His first collection for Givenchy, inspired by the legend of Jason and the Argonauts, had seemed to caricature both the myth and the haute-couture process in a heavy-handed execution. However, by the spring of 1998 McQueen had

THIS PAGE AND OPPOSITE: THE RUNWAY AND BACKSTAGE AT THE ALEXANDER MCQUEEN FOR GIVENCHY HAUTE-COUTURE SPRING/ SUMMER 1998 COLLECTION, PHOTOGRAPHED BY ANNE DENIAU

absorbed and refined his approach. He would later say, 'At Givenchy I learned lightness ... I learned to soften. For me, it was an education ... working in the atelier was fundamental to my career.' It is without doubt this collection that shows that defining moment when McQueen finally understood the possibilities of haute couture. While his collections for Givenchy were by no means his strongest, they allowed him to see the possibilities of that lightness and the way in which the skilled work of the *petites mains* (see also pages 86–91) could bring about an entirely different feel to his design process. Immediately after seeing the collection, fashion journalist Suzy Menkes noted, 'The overriding impression was how hard McQueen had worked to turn his signatures into something special,' and the 'Zen-like calm' she referred to was yet another departure for McQueen. Far from the dark inspirations of serial killers, Jacobean Scotland and Edgar Allan Poe that had defined his previous collections, there was a lightness and romanticism within his latest Givenchy offering.

The Spring/Summer 1998 collection had at its heart the evocative language of Japonisme and McQueen's palette, execution and detail were far more in keeping with the haute couture and Orientalism of the early twentieth-century French designer Paul Poiret, as well as a fresh and entirely innovative vision of the *belle époque*. He had grasped delicacy and fantasy rather than harnessed brutality and, in so doing, made the leap from being a skilled and impulsive designer to being a master couturier. This dress, in the palest dove-grey silk crepe and embroidered with chainmail by the legendary house of François Lesage, holds the signature of McQueen, with its high collar, tightly capped sleeves and undulating bias. However, it also contains within it a finesse and a romanticism that heralded a new chapter for McQueen.

Despite the collection being better received, it was viewed by many as pleasant but rather safe. While blame was focused on McQueen, more should have been laid at the door of the house of Givenchy. In 2001, amid bitter argument, revenge cancellations of shows and a sale to Gucci Group of the controlling interest in McQueen's own label, his tenure at Givenchy came to an end. The fabled couture atelier founded by a French aristocrat and made immortal by the classic haute couture created for Audrey Hepburn had failed to find a new incarnation. McQueen was one of a series of designers who had tried to reinterpret the house and not succeeded, including John Galliano before him and Julien Macdonald after him. As McQueen himself said, 'I could never grasp the Audrey Hepburn of Givenchy because I could never see that that person really existed.'

Following his departure from Givenchy, McQueen focused entirely on his own house. Armed with a deeper understanding of the haute-couture process, the global client and the machinations of corporate structure, the house of McQueen became a world leader in the twenty-first-century design aesthetic. His unique combination of honesty and fantasy was paired with an even more finely honed approach, and where before was only darkness, he was able to flit between night and day and dream and nightmare in equal measure. In 2003 Alexander McQueen was awarded the title Commander of the Most Excellent Order of the British Empire (CBE) by Her Majesty The Queen, named British Designer of the Year for the fourth time (having previously won in 1996, 1997 and 2001) and was also named International Designer of the Year by the Council of Fashion Designers of America. The *enfant terrible*

had grown up, and while he may still have been *terrible* on occasion, his extraordinary vision had placed him at the apex of the fashion world.

While the fashion house of Alexander McQueen was thriving, the man behind it was crumbling. Still grieving over the suicide, in 2007, of the magazine editor Isabella Blow, his closest friend and the woman who discovered him, McQueen suffered a further loss when his beloved mother Joyce died in 2010. Sharing an incredibly close relationship with her son, Joyce was always seated on the front row of his shows and he considered her his greatest ally and most trusted advisor. McQueen was devastated by her death from cancer and, combined with the suicide of his mentor Isabella, seemingly could take no more. Only nine days after his mother's death, the extraordinarily talented, unique and vulnerable designer Alexander McQueen committed suicide.

OPPOSITE: THE WILLIAMVINTAGE ALEXANDER MCQUEEN FOR GIVENCHY HAUTE-COUTURE DRESS BEING SEEN FOR THE FIRST TIME UPON THE SPRING/SUMMER 1998 RUNWAY, PHOTOGRAPHED BY ANNE DENIAU

The McQueen Legacy

McQueen

Dior

Pam Hogg

Mugler

The Modern Femme Fatale

ABOVE: THE SUPERMODELS ESTELLE LEFÉBURE,
LINDA EVANGELISTA, NADJA AUERMANN AND
TYRA BANKS WEARING THIERRY MUGLER IN
GEORGE MICHAEL'S 'TOO FUNKY' VIDEO, 1992

OPPOSITE: A WILLIAMVINTAGE THIERRY MUGLER
BALL GOWN IN PALE PINK DUCHESSE SILK, 1999

*Above all other designers,
THIERRY MUGLER managed
to convey the excess of the 1980s
alongside an attention to tailoring
that went on to define the 1990s.*

The 1980s saw huge changes in fashion. Artistically, culturally and commercially, the resonance of fashion had grown immensely, and being able to express oneself through what one chose to wear was no longer the preserve of the rich and famous. From the punk of Vivienne Westwood and Malcolm McLaren, the New Romanticism of Leigh Bowery and Susan Clowes, the ebullient haute couture of Christian Lacroix, and the excesses of Arnold Scaasi and Roberto Capucci, to the fashion revolutions of Patrick Kelly and Jean Paul Gaultier, the role of fashion had altered dynamically. While 1980s fashion is often oversimplified as puffball skirts, shoulder pads and primary colours, it was a time when there had never been so many sartorial tribes with which to align oneself. As the decade drew to a close, the cleaner, more sophisticated lines of Claude Montana, Donna Karan and Azzedine Alaïa grew in popularity, paving the way for the structured minimalism that was to be the response to a decade of such attention-grabbing, frantic excess.

One designer above all others managed to convey both the lascivious extravagance of the 1980s and the club-kid luxury of the boom decade alongside a sharpness of line and attention to tailoring that would define the 1990s; this was Thierry Mugler. Born in Alsace in 1948, Mugler attended the Strasbourg School of Decorative Arts before training as a ballet dancer. The tall, lithe and incredibly handsome youth left the corps de ballet of the Rhine Opera in 1968 and after a period working freelance in America, Paris and London as a window dresser, costume designer and fashion designer, he established his own house in 1975. Mugler first came to the attention of the fashion world in the July 1977 issue of *Vogue* in a feature entitled 'New Designers ... New Ideas'.

The house of Mugler was known for an adoration of the female form, considered by some to be as misogynistic and idolatry as that of Dior in the 1940s and 1950s, with wasp waists, enhanced shoulders and exaggerated bustlines, and an ideal of the ultimate woman as powerful, magical and, above all else, deeply sexual. His work fused leather, silk, vinyl, velvet and mesh within a context and silhouette of an empowered, brazenly feminine woman. By 1984 Mugler was a fashion

superstar. His Spring/Summer couture show was held in a concert hall in Paris with an audience of over four-thousand.

As the decade came to an end and the 1990s began, Mugler became synonymous with not just a specific approach to fashion but also a specific approach to life: decadent, bacchanalian and grounded in luxury. This dress, an extremely rare example of a Mugler ball gown in palest pink silk with a vast train, internal bustle, the signature Mugler 'wings' to its bust and set with mesh illusion panels, exemplifies the life of a particular kind of woman in the 1990s. The club kids and punks of the 1980s were now in their twenties and thirties, and Mugler offered a refuge for the wealthy who did not want to turn into their parents just because they had turned twenty-one. Princess Gloria von Thurn und Taxis, better known as 'The Punk Princess' or 'TNT', was a young, aristocratic and supremely wealthy woman who partied everywhere from New York's Bowery and Meatpacking Districts to the Venice Biennale and who saw in Mugler a unique language perfect for her life. Equally, Mugler caught the eye of the more mature woman who did not want to retire into a wardrobe of Chanel suits and Oscar de la Renta simply because she had reached a certain age. There was no better exemplar of this than Ivana Trump, the beautiful former

ABOVE: IVANA TRUMP AND JEFF STRYKER IN THE THIERRY MUGLER RUNWAY SHOW, AUTUMN/WINTER 1992

OPPOSITE: EMMA SJÖBERG WEARING THE MOTORBIKE BODICE IN THE THIERRY MUGLER RUNWAY SHOW, AUTUMN/WINTER 1992

Olympic skier. Following her marriage and subsequent headline-grabbing divorce from Donald Trump, the richest man in Manhattan, Ivana became one of the most iconic women of the 1980s and 1990s; a time when conspicuous consumption, capitalism and the power suit reached their zenith.

If a fashion house can be seen to have a golden year, for the house of Mugler it was without question 1992, when the Mugler sensibility extended itself far outside of fashion for the first time. At the height of both the MTV era and the Supermodel decade that saw Naomi, Linda, Cindy, Christy, Claudia and Nadja – each of whom modelled for Mugler – become household names, Thierry Mugler directed George Michael's 'Too Funky' music video. A parody of a real Mugler show, the video features Linda Evangelista, Nadja Auermann, Emma Sjöberg and Tyra Banks, amongst a cast of other celebrated models, each of whom is clad in Mugler. The video, one of the most iconic reference points for the 1990s, was the Mugler brand of fashion, sex and rock'n'roll brought to life.

In a further extension of the Mugler brand and a definitive move away from using merely models and supermodels to express his design sensibility, Mugler's Spring/Summer show of 1992 featured not only Naomi and Nadja but also the musicians Lady Miss Kier and DJ Dmitry of Deee-Lite, his devoted client Ivana Trump and, extraordinarily, the porn star Jeff Stryker, who stripped out of skintight Mugler trousers on stage to reveal a pair of leather briefs emblazoned with 'Lucky Me' on the rear, no doubt a reference to his legendary endowment. The house of Mugler had positioned itself as the brand of choice for the rich and confident, and aligned itself with the worlds of music, cinema and sex as well as fashion.

Now a global brand with a designer as famous as his clothing and with influence in so many arenas, Mugler launched its first perfume, Angel, during the same year. With its heady combination of patchouli and chocolate, the perfume was a perfect, evocative extension of the house message. By 1998 it was the first perfume to replace Chanel Number 5 as the world's bestselling fragrance and by 2013 sales of Angel and its derivatives exceeded $250,000,000.

Thierry Mugler and his house may have been the voice of the Amazonian woman at the height of the 1990s, but behind the roles of dominatrix, vamp, robot and doll that Mugler idealised, and despite his protestations that he was a modernist who never looked to the past, when viewing pieces from his collection something is remarkably clear. Stripped of the accompanying soundtracks, of the bold

accessories and make-up of the era, and of the iconic models, porn stars and celebrities he used to showcase his clothes, the house of Mugler was at its heart obsessed with the notion of French '*tailleur*'. His separates, suits and gowns all have at their core an in-depth and expert understanding of the golden age of French haute couture. Their sense of proportion is not born of an intense new modernism but is without doubt based upon the masterpieces of the late 1940s to early 1950s, with precisely cut panels, sharp waists, exaggerated silhouettes, superb seamwork and an almost supernatural understanding of cloth, evocative of the work of both Elsa Schiaparelli and Charles James.

This ball gown may be redolent of Thierry Mugler and of everything his house stood for in 1999, on the cusp of the new millennium, but its language is just as much that of Old Hollywood and of the great couturiers of the late 1950s. As such, it is the perfect expression of an intensely talented designer who absorbed a message within the cloth and, rather than replicate it, translated it for a whole new generation of women. Hidden within the design revolutionary was, in fact, a great classicist.

PREVIOUS PAGE LEFT: A JEAN PATOU HAUTE-COUTURE BALL GOWN, PHOTOGRAPHED BY HENRY CLARKE FOR FRENCH VOGUE, 1955

PREVIOUS PAGE RIGHT: THE WILLIAMVINTAGE THIERRY MUGLER BALL GOWN WORN BY CATHERINE ZETA-JONES AT THE CANNES FILM FESTIVAL, 1999

The Mugler Legacy

Zac Posen   *Oscar de la Renta*   *Marchesa*

Picture Credits

The publisher has made every effort to trace the photographers and copyright holders. We apologise in advance for any unintentional omission, and would be pleased to insert the appropriate acknowledgement in any subsequent edition.

Pages 1, 4, 9, 11, 13, 15, 21, 23, 29, 31, 37, 39, 45, 47, 50, 51, 54, 55, 61, 69, 77, 79, 85, 87, 89, 93, 95, 98, 99, 103, 104, 105, 108, 109, 113, 115, 121, 122, 126, 127, 131, 133, 135, 136, 141, 143, 151, 153, 159, 161, 165, 167, 173, 175, 181, 183 © WilliamVintage

Page 2 © Jean-Baptiste Mondino

Page 6 © Justin Coit from Rachel Zoe's Living in Style

Page 8 © Jackie Dixon

Page 12 © Getty (above); Courtesy of the Library of Congress, LC-USZ62-95353 (below)

Page 14 © Estate of Antonio Lopez & Juan Ramos

Pages 16–17 © The Richard Avedon Foundation

Page 18 © Catwalkpictures.com

Page 19 © Estate of George Platt Lynes

Page 22 © Mark Giarrusso c/o Manhattan Digest (above); © Topfoto (below)

Page 24 Condé Nast Archive/Corbis © 2015 The Estate of Edward Steichen/ARS, NY and DACS

Page 26 (left to right) © Catwalkpictures.com; © Getty; © Getty; © Catwalkpictures.com

Page 27 Condé Nast Archive/Corbis © 2015 The Estate of Edward Steichen/ARS, NY and DACS

Page 30 © Geoffrey Clements/Corbis (above); © Christie's Images/Bridgeman Images (below)

Page 32 © Musée des Beaux-Arts, Nantes, France/Bridgeman Images

Page 33 © Mary Evans Picture Library

Page 34 © Man Ray Trust/ADAGP, Paris and DACS, London 2015

Page 35 © Catwalkpictures.com (left & centre); © Getty (right)

Page 38 Photo courtesy Staley/Wise Gallery © Horst (above); © Melvyn Longhurst/Alamy (centre); © Les Editions Jalou,

L'Officiel, 1935 (below)

Page 40 © 2015 Tamara Art Heritage Licensed by MMI NYC

41 © Michel Arnaud

42 © Getty

43 © Catwalkpictures.com (left & centre); © GoRunway (right)

Page 46 © Bridgeman Images (above); © Bridgeman Images (centre); © National Portrait Gallery, London (below)

Page 48 © Condé Nast Archive/Corbis;

Page 49 (left to right) © Catwalkpictures.com; © GoRunway; © Getty Images

Page 52 © Les Editions Jalou, L'Officiel, 1957

Page 53 (left to right) © Catwalkpictures.com; © GoRunway; © Catwalkpictures.com

Page 56 Photo © National Gallery of Ireland

Page 57 © Condé Nast Archive/Corbis

Page 58 Irving Penn/Vogue © Condé Nast

Page 59 (left to right) © Catwalkpictures.com

Page 62 © Toni Frissell (above); © PA (below)

Page 64 © Barbra Walz

Page 65 Photo by Dick Balarian © Estate of Antonio Lopez & Juan Ramos

Page 66 © Condé Nast Archive/Corbis

Page 67 (left to right) © GoRunway; © Catwalkpictures.com

Page 70 © Harewood House Trust/Bridgeman Images (above); Bridgeman Images (centre); Bridgeman Images (below)

Page 72 © Association Willy Maywald/ADAGP, Paris and DACS, London 2015

Page 73 © Kunsthistorisches Museum, Vienna, Austria/Bridgeman Images

Page 74 (left & right) © Catwalkpictures.com

Page 75 © Mark Shaw/mptvimages.com

Page 80 © Getty

Page 81 © Bettmann/Corbis

Page 82 (left to right) © Catwalkpictures.com; © GoRunway

Page 83 © Association Willy Maywald/ADAGP, Paris and DACS, London 2015

Page 86 Sotheby's (above & below)

Page 88 © Getty

Page 90 © Les Editions Jalou, L'Officiel, 1954

Page 91 (left to right) © Catwalkpictures.com; © GoRunway

Page 94 © Getty (above); © Louvre, Paris/Bridgeman Images (centre); Getty (below)

Page 96 © Les Editions Jalou, L'Officiel, 1952

Page 97 (left to right) © Catwalkpictures.com

Page 100 (left & right) © Catwalkpictures.com

Page 101 © Les Editions Jalou, L'Officiel, 1952

Page 105 © Getty (above); © Corbis (centre); © PA (below)

Page 106 © The Richard Avedon Foundation

Page 110 Irving Penn/Vogue © Condé Nast

Page 111 (left to right) © Rex; © Catwalkpictures.com

Page 114 © Getty (above, centre & below)

Page 116 Bert Stern/Vogue © Condé Nast Inc 1963

Page 117 © Getty

Page 118 William Klein/Vogue © Condé Nast Inc

Page 119 © GoRunway (left); © Catwalkpictures.com (centre); © Catwalkpictures.com (right)

Page 123 © Getty (above, centre & below)

Page 124 © Pat/Stills/Gamma, Camera Press London

Page 125 (left to right) © Catwalkpictures.com

Page 128 © Alain Dejean/Sygma/Corbis

Page 129 (left to right) © Catwalkpictures.com

Page 132 © Balthazar Korab courtesy of The Library of

Congress (above & below)

Page 134 © Getty

Page 137 © Getty

Page 138 (left to right) © Catwalkpictures.com

Page 139 © The Helmut Newton Estate

Page 142 Art Collector/HIP/TopFoto (above); © Eugène Rubin/FNAC/Centre national des arts plastique (below)

Page 144 © Eugene Rubin/Courtesy Biksady Galéria

Pages 146–7 © Guy Bourdin for Vogue Italia, May 1975

Page 148 © Estate of George Platt Lynes

Page 149 (left to right) © Catwalkpictures.com

Page 152 © Heritage Images (above); © Getty (centre); © Getty (centre); © Rex (below)

Page 154 © Getty

Page 155 © Getty (above); © Getty (below)

Page 156 © Harry Benson, 1978

Page 157 (left to right) © Catwalkpictures.com

Page 160 © Rex (above); © Getty (below)

Page 162 (left to right) © Catwalkpictures.com

Page 163 © Getty

Page 166 © The Art Archive/Victoria & Albert Museum London/Sally Chappell (above); © The Art Archive/Ashmolean Museum (centre); © The Art Archive/DeA Picture Library (below)

Page 168 © Les Editions Jalou, L'Officiel, 1955

Page 169 © Condé Nast Archive/Corbis

Page 170 (left to right) © GoRunway

Page 171 © Getty

Page 174 © Man Ray Trust/ADAGP, Paris and DACS, London 2015 (above); © Sotheby's (below)

Pages 176-77 © Anne Deniau

Page 178 (left to right) © Catwalkpictures.com

Page 179 © Anne Deniau

Page 182 © 1992 Sony BMG Music

Index

Acknowledgements

The process of writing *25 Dresses* has been an extraordinary pleasure and this is largely because of the support, creativity and diligence of so many colleagues and friends. I must thank my agent Adrian Sington of DCD Media for first suggesting I write a book and extend that thanks to my marvellous editor Lisa Pendreigh at Quadrille for agreeing with him. To the sterling Quadrille team of Jane O'Shea, Nicola Ellis, Katie Horwich, Ed Griffiths and Margaux Durigon who have made the many months of work a real joy, thank you for being so passionate and for fuelling me with so much chocolate and so many baked goods during the process. To Anna Soderblom and Oliver Reimann, thank you for taking such truly exquisite, dazzling photography of my greatest discoveries and bringing the dresses to life within my book. To Petronella Wyatt, thank you for being an avid 'first reader' of each and every chapter, for your incisive questioning and for the way in which you made me feel my book was a living, breathing entity.

25 Dresses could not have been written without the staunch support of my incredible WilliamVintage team of Elspeth Booth, Georgina Rossi, Rosie Hill, Amy Hill, Alisha Brittan and Mirjam Maraama whose encouragement means so very much and who work alongside me on a daily basis. Their belief in the principles of WilliamVintage and their passion for fine vintage clothing help shape the company I founded and for that I am forever grateful.

I owe an enormous debt of gratitude to the extraordinary directors, stylists, photographers, journalists and editors who have long supported me and who include Alexandra Schulman, Katie Grand, Elizabeth Saltzman, Jo Elvin, Lucinda Chambers, Fiona Golfar, Emma Marsh, Jerry Stafford, Joe McKenna, Elizabeth Stewart, Amanda Harlech and so many more creative geniuses who have helped shape WilliamVintage and inspired me more times than I can begin to count.

I must thank each and every 'WilliamVintage Woman', however, there are far too many to list; to see the dresses contained within this book, and so very many more, find new homes with women who love them, wear them and live life in them is my greatest joy. I must also thank Jacqueline Soppet and Katharina Turner for not only helping shape the company I founded but for helping shape me as a man; not a day goes by without my thinking of you and I hope you are both looking down with a smile on your faces while clad in vintage Dior.

Thank you to my parents, Greta and Wilfred, for their unending support and love and for feeding my passion for the arts since my childhood.

Lastly, I must thank Alexander Hall Taylor. Thank you for being my partner, my best friend and for being the man who makes every day a joy, every week a celebration and every year an adventure. I love you.

PUBLISHING DIRECTOR **JANE O'SHEA**

COMMISSIONING EDITOR **LISA PENDREIGH**

COPY EDITOR **ZIA MATTOCKS**

CREATIVE DIRECTOR **HELEN LEWIS**

DESIGNER **NICOLA ELLIS**

PICTURE RESEARCHER **KATIE HORWICH**

PRODUCTION DIRECTOR **VINCENT SMITH**

PRODUCTION CONTROLLER **SASHA HAWKES**

First published in 2015 by Quadrille Publishing Ltd
Pentagon House, 52–54 Southwark Street, London SE1 1UN
www.quadrille.co.uk

Quadrille is an imprint of Hardie Grant
www.hardiegrant.com.au

Text © 2014 William Banks-Blaney
Design and layout © 2014 Quadrille Publishing Ltd

All rights reserved. No part of this publication may be reproduced, stored in a retrieval system, or transmitted in any form or by any means, electronic, electrostatic, magnetic tape, mechanical, photocopying, recording, or otherwise, without the prior permission in writing of the publisher.

The rights of William Banks-Blaney to be identified as the author of this work have been asserted by him in accordance with the Copyright, Design and Patents Act 1988.

British Library Cataloguing-in-Publication Data
A catalogue record for this book is available from the British Library

ISBN 978 184949 471 7

10 9 8 7 6 5 4 3 2 1

Printed in China